The Chisholm Trail

Cattle drive in Indian Territory. Herds were bedded on high ground to take advantage of the breeze. Courtesy of the Oklahoma Historical Society

The Chisholm Trail

High Road of the Cattle Kingdom

Don Worcester

Indian Head Books

New York

This edition published by Indian Head Books,
a division of Barnes & Noble, Inc.,
by arrangement with the University of Nebraska Press.

1994 Indian Head Books

ISBN 1-56619-397-4

Printed and bound in the United States of America

M 9 8 7 6 5 4 3

Dear SANDY,

Enclosed is the item you purchased through eBay. I hope you are happy with it and we can do business again in the future.

Sincerely,

Sue

Susan Cummings

(suste√@rcn.com - aka "tonto5")

[I sometimes get behind on feedback. If you leave me one, I will immediately leave you one. Thanks.]

ENJOY!

It was a Pleasure doing business with you.

To my son Harris

Contents

Illustrations

Preface

ALTHOUGH THE CHISHOLM TRAIL was open for less than two decades, millions of cattle traveled north over it. More than any of the other trails from Texas, it was the major route of cattle and horses, cowboys and cowmen, to Kansas railheads as well as the new ranches springing up all over the former ranges of the buffalo and the Plains Indians between 1867 and the Big Die-up of 1886–87. In fact, the name *Chisholm Trail* came to be applied indiscriminately to all of the cattle trails north out of Texas. This book is an attempt to portray, in text and photographs, the way of life created by the Chisholm Trail during the period of the great drives.

Although photography was in its early stages of development, some graphic photographs were made of ranch life and the trail before the end of the open-range, free grass era. Cowboy photographers have provided a valuable supplement to the memoirs of cowmen and cowboys. Using simple, often home-made cameras, the complicated wet plate process, and the collodion bottle and bath, they captured cowboys in action as well as at rest.

One of the most successful of the frontier photographers was L. A. Huffman, who arrived in Montana in 1878. A part-time rancher, Huffman was at home in cow camps and on roundups; many of his best photographs were taken from horseback. Two photographer-collectors who preserved valuable collections of old photographs in addition to the ones they took were Fred Mazzulla of Denver, Colorado, and N. H. Rose of Menardville, Texas.

I am grateful to Marni Sandweiss and Dr. Ronnie C. Tyler of the Amon Carter Museum of Western Art, Fort Worth, for their assistance in obtaining and selecting appropriate photographs. My thanks go also to my daughter and son-in-law, Barby and Michael J. Stephen of Helena, Montana, for their help in acquiring photographic and other materials, and to Keith Anderson, also of Helena, for sharing his father's old photographs with me.

Introduction

THE great cattle drives from Texas northward across the plains produced one of the nation's most enduring folk heroes. The cowboy, with his sombrero and lariat, mounted on a half-broken mustang, displaced the forest frontiersman with coonskin cap, squirrel rifle, and faithful hound in the pantheon of American folk heroes. Paradoxically, while the old-time frontiersman had been a free man, his own master, the cowboy was, as W. H. Hutchinson has noted, ever a "hired man on horseback" in the employ of cowman or syndicate. But, Hutchinson adds, "If you think all men are equal, you ain't never been afoot and met a man ridin' a good horse."[1] In the era of the long drives, from the 1860s to the 1890s, the cowboy became a legendary figure.

Trailing cattle was not new; Americans had "walked" cattle to market for more than two centuries, although the herds were small and easily handled by men on foot. A boy led a belled ox down the road and the cattle followed; a few men on foot brought up the rear to keep any from straying. They traveled through farming country and placed the cattle in fenced pastures each night. There was no need for night herding, no danger of stampedes. Fat cattle had been walked from Springfield, Massachusetts, to Boston as early as the 1650s. By the early nineteenth century, cattle were regularly driven from the Ohio valley to markets as distant as New York City.

There was nothing glamorous or captivating about these early cattle drives or the men who made them. While the term *cowboy* was used even before the American Revolution, it conveyed more contempt than respect. If there had been no Longhorns, mustangs, open range, or long drives it is unlikely that cowboys would ever have caught the public's fancy.

When the Civil War ended, an enormous tract of rich grassland in the central and northern plains remained the undisputed domain of warlike nomads whose way of life depended on the buffalo, or American bison. Cattlemen had not yet invaded this vast hunting ground, but as hide hunters decimated the buffalo herds in the next decade, millions of Longhorns from South Texas would take their places. Other cattle entered the northern plains from Oregon and Utah, and "Pilgrim," or farm, cattle were shipped from states east of the Mississippi River. The brief era of open range and free grass generated the greatest cattle boom in world history.

The age of the great cattle drives was one of rapid changes in American life both east and west, many of them stimulated by technological inventions. Eastern factories, developed or enlarged during the Civil War, supported a growing population and contributed to the increasing demand for beef. Railroads, pushing westward across the plains, provided transportation for live cattle to the packing plants of Chicago and St. Louis. Refrigerated railroad cars and ships introduced the dressed-beef trade to eastern and trans-Atlantic markets in the 1870s.[2]

The invention that had the most revolutionary impact on the cattle kingdom was barbed wire, invented by Isaac Ellwood, Joseph Farwell Glidden, and Jacob Haish of De Kalb County, Illinois, in the 1870s. In 1876 John W. ("Bet a Million") Gates demonstrated to skeptical Texas cowmen in San Antonio that the wire would hold Longhorns.[3]

This was one of those moments that bridge a chasm between two vastly different ages. Before Gates's demonstration, the era of open range and free grass was supreme. After it that age of pioneer cowmen was doomed, simply because a bunch of Longhorns had backed away from eight slender strands armed with tiny barbs. No one present foresaw how drastically "bob waire" would transform his way of life within a dozen years. Only gradually did the open-range cowmen realize that they, their Longhorns, and their mustang cow ponies no longer had a place in a land of privately owned and securely fenced pastures.

Wise cowmen began buying land by the section and enclosing it with barbed wire. The severe drouth of 1883 forced many cowmen to seek other grass and water; when they found fences in their way, they reacted angrily. The "Fence War" raged

Rancho Perdido, Jim Wells County, Texas, in 1890. Built in 1871 by Martin Culver. Western History Collections, University of Oklahoma Library

Jesse Chisholm, Cherokee-Scot trader, whose wagon tracks across Indian Territory became known as Chisholm's Trail. Texas cowmen gave his name to the entire trail from San Antonio to Kansas. Courtesy of the Oklahoma Historical Society

sporadically for several years before the Texas Rangers put an end to fence cutting.

In 1879 fencing became a problem in Wyoming, for big outfits like the Anglo-American Cattle Company and Swan Land and Cattle Company enclosed whole sections of public land. In 1883 the secretary of the interior authorized settlers to destroy fences that were in their way to land they wished to homestead. Two years later Congress outlawed fences on federal lands, and President Grover Cleveland ordered them removed.[4] Northern ranchers gradually purchased and fenced their ranges, although the free grass era lasted longer in parts of Montana.

The six-shooter and repeating rifle were inventions that helped convert the central and northern grasslands from the buffalo range of the plains Indians to a major part of the cattle kingdom. By facilitating the extermination of the buffalo herds, these guns helped destroy the basis for the plains nomads' way of life, reducing them to the status of wards of the government. With the removal of these two obstacles to Anglo occupation of the plains, the cattle kingdom spread from South Texas to Montana and the Dakotas in less than a decade. "For every single buffalo that roamed the Plains in 1871," Richard Irving Dodge wrote, "there are in 1881 not less than two, and more probably four or five, of the descendants of the long-horned cattle of Texas. The destroyers of the buffalo are followed by the preservers of the cattle."[5]

The rapid spread of the cattle ranges occurred as millions of surplus animals were herded north from Texas. The oldest of the northern routes was the Shawnee Trail from San Antonio past Austin, Waco, and Dallas, fording the Red River at Rock Bluff near Preston. It passed through the Indian Nations, the lands of the Five Civilized Tribes, to Baxter Springs, Kansas, or Sedalia, Missouri. Most of the cattle driven up the Shawnee Trail were destined for feed lot or market rather than for stocking new ranches.

The routes by which most of the stock cattle reached the northern ranges were the Chisholm Trail to central Kansas and the later Western Trail to Dodge City. Of all the Texas cattle routes, the Chisholm Trail was the most used and by far the best known. Its name came from Scot-Cherokee Indian trader Jesse Chisholm, who in 1865 began hauling trade goods in wagons from his post near the future site of Wichita, Kansas, to Indian camps on the North Canadian River, about 220 miles to the south. Other parts of the trail were at first called by various names, but Texas trail men soon applied Chisholm's name to the entire route from San Antonio to Abilene and later Kansas shipping points. The "Chisholm Trail" was mentioned in Kansas newspapers in the spring of 1870, and in Texas papers by 1874.[6]

From South Texas, herds heading for the Shawnee and Chisholm trails followed the same landmarks toward San Antonio, San Marcos, or Austin. Near Waco the Shawnee Trail swung toward Dallas, while the Chisholm Trail continued north to Cleburne and Fort Worth. Beyond Fort Worth it followed along near the route of modern Highway 81, past Decatur to Red River Station, and over the sites of the future Oklahoma towns of Duncan, Chickasha, El Reno, and Enid. It crossed into Kansas where Caldwell was built as a trading post for trail crews in 1871. The trail swerved east of Jesse Chisholm's trading post, past the future site of Newton, and on to Abilene. Although Abilene was the first terminus of the Chisholm Trail, after 1871 the end of the trail might be any of several Kansas cowtowns, among them Ellsworth, Junction City, Newton, Wichita, and Caldwell. Even though most of the cattle were trailed on to the north or west of these towns, none of the northern routes was named after Jesse Chisholm.

All of the major trails were broad and general, not narrow lanes, and many minor trails joined them along the way. Cowmen using these feeder trails often gave them the name of the major trail they joined, adding to the confusion. Wayne Gard compared the Chisholm Trail to a tree: the roots were the feeder trails, the trunk was the main route from San Antonio across Indian Territory, and the branches were the extensions to the various railheads in Kansas.[7] When only a few herds were following a trail, they usually found adequate forage close by. But when many herds were on the move during any season, the later ones had to travel parallel to the tracks of the earlier ones to find

MAJOR CATTLE TRAILS

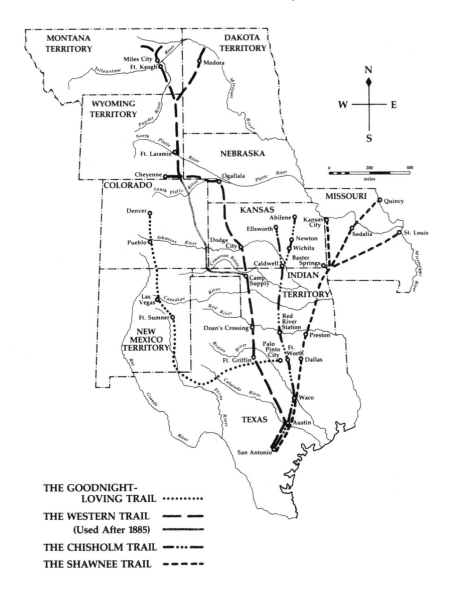

THE GOODNIGHT-
LOVING TRAIL ⋯⋯⋯⋯

THE WESTERN TRAIL — —
(Used After 1885) ▬▬▬

THE CHISHOLM TRAIL —⋯—

THE SHAWNEE TRAIL — — —

grass. The drying up of streams and waterholes also caused variations in the route.

The Chisholm Trail was widely known by name, and the name was often applied indiscriminately to any route cattle might follow out of Texas.[8] Most of the men who used the trail probably had never heard of Jesse Chisholm or his wagon road; many thought it was named for Texan John Chisum, who trailed cattle to New Mexico. Some people even today restrict the use of the name Chisholm to the part of the trail he actually used. But since cowmen who followed the trail applied Chisholm's name to the entire distance from San Antonio to the Kansas railheads, there is no compelling reason to overrule them a century later.[9] No one even knows, after all, how or why the Shawnee Trail got its name.

The western myth that arose in the era of open range, free grass, and long drives has retained its vitality because, as C. L. Sonnichsen noted, our "basic need is a natural and normal hunger for a heroic past. . . . All we have to fill this basic need is 25 years between 1865 and 1890. It was something of a heroic age, and we have done our best to make it one." And, he added, "When we remember that the legendary West belongs to the world and not just to us, the subject assumes major importance."[10]

For two decades trail bosses, cooks, and cowboys followed Longhorns up the Chisholm Trail, unaware they were creating a "legendary West" that would long outlive the open range and the cattle kingdom. Their story is told in the following pages.

The Chisholm Trail

Modern Longhorn steers on the Wichita Wildlife Refuge, Oklahoma.
Photo by E. P. Haddon for the Bureau of Sport Fisheries and Wildlife.
Western History Collections, University of Oklahoma Library

CHAPTER 1

Cow Poor

Other states were carved or born
Texas grew from hide and horn.
Breta Hart Nance, "Cattle"

TEXAS had been a land of cattle and horses ever since the Spaniards introduced them in the seventeenth century. Anglo-Americans arriving in Texas after 1800 found thousands of Spanish cattle and countless wild horses, or mustangs (from *mesteño,* meaning a stray or ownerless animal). Anglos also brought livestock, which mixed with the native stock to produce the longhorns of South Texas. A German who traveled widely in Texas in 1849 differentiated between American and Mexican cattle, saying, "The former is tamer, the latter tends to become wild."[1] Other visitors, both earlier and later, commented on the long horns of the cattle they saw.

Longhorns were a robust breed of many colors—black, red, roan, white, brindled, yellow, and various combinations. They were long of leg and hard of hoof, perfectly adapted to the region, able to travel for grass and water and defend themselves against predators. They had developed an immunity to the tick fever that proved fatal to other cattle, but unfortunately they carried the ticks wherever they went. The Longhorns of the brush country were as wild and wary as any living creature, more difficult to stalk and kill than deer or buffalo. They roamed in scattered bands of perhaps half a dozen, hiding in the brush by day, coming out to graze at night.

Not all Texas cattle were Longhorns, nor were all immune to tick fever. The cattle of central and North Texas, which were a mixture of Shorthorns brought from the East or South and native or Spanish stock, were susceptible to the disease. Charles Goodnight described them as dark, line-backed, mealy-nosed,

3

round-barreled, and well formed. Like the Longhorns, they easily became wild and difficult to handle, even dangerous.[2]

Anglos also brought Thoroughbreds and Quarter Horses,
which they raised at first for racing. Eventually both were crossed with little mustang mares to produce larger and swifter cow
horses. For many years, however, the mustang cow pony and the
Longhorn were inseparable elements of the Texas cattle industry. Together they made the era of the long drives possible.

Although after the Civil War Texas was the unrivaled source
of cattle, before the war the Five Civilized Tribes of Indian Territory raised and exported thousands of cattle to states to the
north and east. The Cherokees, Choctaws, Chickasaws, Creeks,
and Seminoles had learned open range cattle raising and trailing
livestock to market on the southern frontier. Their trade with
Missouri and Illinois antedated that of Texans by only a few
years at most. The cattle the tribes brought to Indian Territory
were apparently of good quality and, according to observers,
"attained great size." By 1847 a regular trade had developed
with buyers from Missouri, Illinois, and Indiana.[3]

During the Civil War both the Union and Confederate ar-
mies as well as other whites looted the herds of Indian Territory.
The depleted herds were gradually rebuilt after the war to an
estimated 700,000 by 1884. Trade with the states to the north
was resumed, but, since these cattle were not carriers of tick
fever, the traffic received little notice.[4]

Spaniards had trailed Texas cattle to Louisiana and northern Mexico in the eighteenth century. In the 1830s, Anglo cowmen drove small herds to New Orleans, and in the following
decade they trailed cattle to Missouri, Ohio, and California.[5] By
1842 many men drove herds across Indian Territory for sale to
army contractors who supplied Forts Smith, Gibson, Scott, and
other military posts. These were fairly profitable years for some
Texas cowmen.

By the early 1850s, Texans trailed cattle to Arkansas, Illinois,
Kansas, Nebraska, Missouri, and Iowa. Illinois feeders regularly
fattened Texas cattle during the decade, and hundreds of Longhorn steers were sold to freighters and farmers to be worked as

oxen. Kansas City became a market for Texas beef, and some Texas cattle were trailed on to Chicago.

In 1853 Tom Candy Ponting and a partner came from Illinois to buy Texas cattle. In preparation for the drive they purchased a wagon, a canvas cover that also served as a tent, and a yoke of oxen. They bought six hundred steers and drove them across the Red River; the steers followed a belled ox that was tied to the back of the wagon. In Indian Territory they bought eighty more prime steers weighing about twelve hundred pounds for nine dollars a head. It took four months to reach Illinois.

After wintering the cattle they trailed 150 of them to Muncie, Indiana, then shipped them by rail to New York City, where beeves brought high prices. It had cost two dollars a head to trail the cattle fifteen hundred miles from Texas; it cost seventeen dollars a head to ship them six hundred miles to New York City. In the spring of 1855 Ponting and his partner sold some of their cattle in Chicago, too. In 1854 George Jackson Squires also went from Illinois to Texas for cattle. He bought five hundred Longhorns near Houston, drove them to Illinois, and later sold them in Chicago.[6]

Texans also trailed cattle to the California mining regions. In 1856 Frederick Law Olmsted saw near San Antonio a herd of four hundred steers heading west under a crew of twenty-five men, all mounted on mules. Most of the riders were working for their keep and transportation to the gold fields. They were five or six months on the trail, but a steer costing fourteen dollars in Texas brought one hundred dollars in California.

In the early days of cattle trailing, oxen hauled carts or wagons that carried bedding and supplies, mainly cornmeal and bacon. If an ox went lame, the men roped a steer and yoked it to the wagon. The food supply was never adequate, and the men usually had nothing to eat but beef before they reached their destination. Fortunately, the herds usually picked up strays along the way, for, as every Texas cowman knew, eating your own beef would make you sick.

Before the Civil War most trail herds numbered only a few hundred head, with four riders for each one hundred cattle.

The men usually had only two or three horses apiece, and these were often thin and sore-backed before the drive ended. Without tents or raincoats, the cowboys were at the mercy of the elements day and night. A man who was separated from the wagon overnight slept on a "Tucson bed"—stomach for a mattress and back for a cover.

The Shawnee Trail became hazardous for trail men and their herds even before the Civil War, for in 1855 an outbreak of "Texas fever" in Missouri killed thousands of cattle. The disease was correctly attributed to the arrival of Longhorns from Texas, but the trouble was blamed on the Longhorns' breath rather than on the ticks that carried the disease. The Missouri legislature banned Texas cattle, and irate Missouri farmers turned back Texas herds the next year. Some cattle crossed eastern Kansas to Kansas City and St. Joseph, and some reached Illinois, but similar epidemics of tick fever in Kansas also led to a quarantine against Texas Longhorns. In 1857, nevertheless, Jesse Day and Willis McCutcheon both trailed herds to Quincy, Illinois, where they sold them profitably. In 1858 Oliver Loving reached Illinois with a herd from his ranch in Palo Pinto County. The following year he wintered a herd in southern Kansas; in the spring of 1860 he drove it up the Arkansas River to Pueblo, Colorado.[7]

During the Civil War the populations of frontier areas in Texas, such as Parker, Palo Pinto, Denton, Wise, and San Saba counties, declined drastically, so that by 1866 no more than one-fifth of the old ranches were still occupied. When both state and Confederate forces were withdrawn after the war, frontier families were left defenseless against Comanche and Kiowa raiders, who ran off thousands of Texas cattle to trade to the Comancheros of New Mexico. Many men gave up the struggle and abandoned their ranches, but others, like the Lovings and Slaughters, moved their families to safety and remained with their cattle.[8]

When trailing cattle resumed, some Anglo cattlemen were not particular about whose animals were in their herds, and rustlers became active as the value of cattle rose. On one occasion some northwest Texas cowmen caught up with a thief who was driving off their cattle. They ate supper with him, then announced that they intended to hang him.

"Boys," he said, "I'll not argue with you, I'll not deny my guilt or ask for mercy. You know me and I know you. I want at least one honest man to have a part in my hanging. Now I want the one of you who never stole a cow to step forward and put the noose around my head." A moment of shocked silence followed, then laughter. They let him go with a warning.[9] Other cow thieves did not get off so lightly when caught, but most were never apprehended.

Many Texans served in the Confederate Army, leaving ranchers short-handed, unable to brand all of their calves or to prevent their cattle from straying. It became customary at this time to look out for others' cattle at branding time; when cows from distant ranges were found, their calves received the mothers' brands. When the branding was finished, these strays were pushed as far as possible toward their own ranges. As long as only honest cattlemen were involved, such customs worked fairly well, but many a Confederate veteran or his widow discovered that his cattle had disappeared. There were, nevertheless, thousands of unbranded cattle; by custom these belonged to the man who burned his brand in their hides and notched his mark in their ears.

In 1865 returning cowmen organized wild cow hunts to replenish their herds, and the great era of "mavericking" began. The term *maverick* came to mean an unmarked stray that was presumed to be ownerless. The name, which spread over the West, arose after Samuel A. Maverick received a herd of stock cattle as a debt settlement and had them driven to a range on the San Antonio River. The man in charge of the cattle neglected to brand the calves. In 1855 Maverick sold the brand and his rights to Toutant de Beauregard, who agreed to hunt and brand the strays. Like later maverickers, Beauregard made the most of the opportunity, rounding up and branding as "Maverick's" all the unbranded cattle he found in a number of surrounding counties.[10]

W. S. James, an old-time Texas cowboy-turned-preacher who had "seen the elephant and heard the owl," wrote a book about life on the range to correct the errors in many books about the West. He thoroughly disapproved of mavericking and the scramble for unbranded cattle that it encouraged. The consequence was, he said, that the more successful men persuaded the legislature to enact laws that made it illegal to brand a calf one did not own. "There began the battle that for years waged unceasingly until the big fish swallowed up the little ones. We had as a result the cattle king and the common cow-puncher. The real difference being that the king no longer had to do his own stealing, for he was able to hire the cow-puncher to do it for him, and if the poor cow-puncher presumed to steal a little scrub for himself once in a while the king wouldn't kick unless someone tried to raise a fuss about it. If he could settle it without too much noise he would do it, and thus add one more link to the poor boy's chains with which to hold him in line. If there was too much noise about it, the king turned honest and sent him down East to work for Texas."

There were, James admitted, honest exceptions, but this is what mavericking generally produced. "When the business first began there were men with cattle who had never stolen, that really believed they were forced to do as other men in self-defense, who began taking lessons in stealing and wound up in the penitentiary. Some became wealthy and, thanks to true manhood, we are able to record that some men preferred to let poverty enter their home than that truth and honesty of purpose be dispossessed of their legitimate throne."[11]

The successful cattlemen, James added, perhaps in bitterness because he had not been one of them, were usually the ones who tended to the business of branding mavericks and looking after the ones they had already branded. "Show me a man who began in the cattle business as early as '68 or '70 who did not go busted, who can truthfully say that he never ate stray beef, never branded cattle whose ownership was questionable, and I will show you a man too good for Texas or Chicago."[12]

To James, "of all the contemptible cow thieves on earth it is the old donker who has stolen himself into respectability and then with his thieving old carcass togged up in a $50 suit of clothes bought with his ill-gotten gains to see him stacked up on a jury to try some boy for stealing a $5 yearling."[13]

Problems other than mavericking troubled Texas ranchers, for even though by 1866 many men had cattle to sell, all the markets were doubtful at best. During the war a few cowmen like Oliver Loving, Dan Waggoner, and Jesse L. Driskill had trailed herds east to supply the Confederate Army, while others had driven cattle to New Orleans. In the early years of the war Confederate money was accepted all over Texas. Later the only ones to profit were those who sold beeves to Union forces in New Orleans after the city fell, for they were paid in gold. The others still received Confederate currency, which soon went out of style.

One of the pioneer long drives was that of Nelson Story, a former overland freighter who followed gold seekers to Virginia City, Montana. Beef was scarce in Montana; in 1866 Story rode to Texas and bought a herd of mixed cattle for ten dollars a head and started them north. He and his men and the cattle survived a multitude of obstacles and hazards, man-made as well as natural. Story sold some of his cattle for a handsome profit and started a ranch with the rest.[14]

In 1866, Oliver Loving and Charles Goodnight pioneered a trail to New Mexico from northwest Texas by way of the future site of San Angelo to the Horsehead Crossing of the Pecos. The scarcity of water as well as Mescalero and Comanche attacks made the route hazardous. Goodnight returned to Texas for more cattle, while Loving drove the herd on to Colorado. Before Loving died of wounds inflicted by the Comanches, the two men had driven a number of herds to Fort Sumner, New Mexico, as well as to Colorado. They were the first Texans to establish a ranch in eastern New Mexico, in the Bosque Grande south of Fort Sumner.

In 1866 Texans drove upwards of two hundred thousand cattle to the north, east, or west, but few of them made profitable sales. Armed men met herds on the Shawnee Trail at the Kansas and Missouri borders and stopped them. Although a few men managed to evade the blockades and find buyers in Iowa and

Early-day Kansas rancher and dugout cabin. Western History Collections, University of Oklahoma Library

elsewhere, others lost most of their cattle. Dan Waggoner sold twenty-five hundred steers in Sedalia, but his was one of the last herds to get through.[15] One trail boss who was forced to turn his herd west at the Kansas line succinctly expressed the feelings of many Texans. In Kansas, he said, there was nothing but "sunshine, sunflowers, and sons-of-bitches."

Among the few successful drovers were two young men who, with the help of twenty cowboys, started a herd from central Texas to their home state of Iowa in April. In crossing the Brazos they lost most of their cooking equipment. At that "all hands gave the Brazos one good harty dam" and continued on their way. They went by way of Baxter Springs and Council Grove, reaching Nebraska City in September. From Ottumwa, Iowa, they shipped the cattle to Chicago.[16]

Captain E. B. Millett turned east at Baxter Springs, but by the time he reached the Mississippi his cattle were in poor condition and virtually unsalable. Millett drove them on to central Illinois, where he wintered them. He sold the herd in the spring, but not profitably. He concluded that there was no money to be made by trailing Texas cattle, but after the Chisholm Trail was opened he changed his mind and drove many herds north. Men who found no other outlet for their cattle sold them to the coastal slaughterhouses to be killed for hides and tallow. Cattle disposed of in this way brought their owners about three dollars a head at best. Texas cowmen, up to their briskets in cattle for which there was no profitable or stable market, faced ruin.

At this critical moment a young cattle dealer of Springfield, Illinois, Joseph G. McCoy, purchased some cattle that W. W. Sugg had brought from Texas in 1866. McCoy shipped his cattle to eastern markets, where they sold readily for high prices. The American population was rising, and the growing demand for beef exceeded the supply. McCoy was one of several men who were determined to meet that demand, but first he had to locate a dependable supply of cattle at reasonable prices.

Charles F. Gross, who in 1865 had surveyed a route for a military telegraph line from Shreveport, Louisiana, to Brownsville, told McCoy where he could find the cattle. He had, Gross said, seen thousands of cattle along the Texas coast "running wild and waiting for someone to gather them and drive them to the northern market."

Sugg confirmed the great numbers of cattle in South Texas and the low prices they brought. He also warned McCoy about the difficulties that drovers encountered on the old Shawnee Trail into eastern Kansas and Missouri. McCoy immediately sensed that a bonanza awaited the man who could find a way to deliver low-cost Texas cattle to eastern markets. The main problem was getting cattle safely to some railhead not under quarantine. At first he considered receiving cattle on the Arkansas River near Fort Smith, where they could be shipped by river or by rail. Other men had similar ideas, but none that proved effective.

In Kansas City, McCoy talked to Marsh and Coffey, who traded for cattle in Indian Territory and along the Red River. They suggested central Kansas as a possible shipping point, for the Eastern Division of the Union Pacific Railroad (later the Kansas and Pacific) had laid tracks westward as far as Salina, Kansas. The Kansas quarantine law applied only to the settled area, leaving the lands to the west open to Texas cattle. Marsh and Coffey warned McCoy, however, that shipping costs from central or western Kansas might leave no profit margin on the cattle. Much depended on railroad freight rates.

When McCoy approached the Union Pacific freight agent at Wyandotte, Kansas, he found the man interested and cooperative. The agent gave him a railroad pass to Salina. On the return trip McCoy had the train stop in Abilene, a hamlet of one-room cabins, two saloons, a post office, a blacksmith shop, a six-room hotel, and a sawhorse beside the railroad track that served as a platform on the rare occasions when the train stopped to discharge passengers.

Because it was unusual for a train to stop in Abilene, almost everyone in town came to see who had arrived. McCoy found them more receptive to his project than anyone elsewhere. He learned that there was plenty of low-priced land available for corrals and shipping pens.

The train also stopped at Junction City, east of Abilene, but although its location was satisfactory, the price of land was too high. While dining there at the Hale House, McCoy discussed his project with Colonel J. J. Myers, a well-known cattleman from Lockhart, Texas, who urged him to put his plans into operation as quickly as possible.

Remembering the warning of Marsh and Coffey, McCoy went to St. Louis to discuss freight rates with officials of several railroad companies, but met mild interest, indifference, or hostility. Union Pacific officials doubted the feasibility of his program, but agreed to let him proceed at his own expense, promising to pay him one-eighth of the freight charges on each carload of cattle shipped, about five dollars. The president of the Missouri Pacific replied to McCoy's question about freight rates by ordering him out of the office. The freight agent of the Hannibal and St. Louis Railroad promised reasonable rates to Chicago, where the Union Stockyards had been built in 1865. As a result of these meetings, Chicago rather than St. Louis became the primary market for Texas cattle.

Kansas quarantine law banned Texas cattle east of a line approximately sixty miles west of Abilene. Fortunately for McCoy, the governor of Kansas was convinced of the benefits the cattle trade would bring and was willing to overlook a minor violation of the quarantine law. "I regard the opening of that cattle trail into and across Western Kansas," Governor Crawford announced, "of as much value to the state as is the Missouri River."[17] McCoy immediately set about making his shipping pens a reality.

There was need for haste, for it was already June, midway through the season for trailing cattle. McCoy bought 250 acres northeast of Abilene and persuaded the railroad to build a siding that would hold one hundred cattle cars. Aware that only the strongest fences would stop Longhorns, he built his shipping pens and corrals of railroad ties. Work on the pens began on July 1, and in two months they were ready for one thousand cattle, with facilities for weighing and for loading forty cattle cars in two hours. Construction of the three-story Drover's Cottage and a bank also got under way.

Farmers east of Abilene protested McCoy's cattle business until they learned that trail bosses were willing to pay high prices for eggs, potatoes, onions, corn, and hay. "If I can make money out of the Texas trade," said the leader of the opposition, "I'm not afraid of Texas fever but if I can't, I'm damned afraid of it."

Although the trailing season was well advanced, McCoy sent handbills to Texas towns and advertisements to newspapers, informing cattlemen of the new market at Abilene. He also sent riders to tell trail bosses who were holding herds in Indian Territory because they knew of no place to sell them. By mid-August a herd that northern cattlemen had bought in Indian Territory was grazing near Abilene, waiting for the pens to be completed.

The first herd that came directly from Texas to Abilene was owned and managed by Colonel O. O. Wheeler and two partners. Wheeler had been driving cattle from southern California to San Francisco, but a drouth had greatly reduced herds. He went to San Antonio, and with his partners purchased twenty-four hundred Longhorn steers and one hundred cow ponies. They hired fifty-four cowboys, arming them with Colt revolvers and Henry repeating rifles, for there was great danger of Indian attacks on the southern plains.

Wheeler and his partners drove their herd along the old Shawnee Trail, leaving it when it swung east toward Dallas. They continued on past Fort Worth and across the Red River. In Indian Territory they came upon Jesse Chisholm's wagon tracks and followed them. Wheeler planned to winter the cattle in Kansas and then drive them through South Pass to San Francisco.

Abilene proved to be the last stop for Wheeler's herd, for his partners, fearing cholera as well as Indian attack, refused to continue. To Wheeler's disgust they shipped the cattle to Chicago from McCoy's pens. Because there had been frequent rains the grass was poor and the lean cattle did not bring a satisfactory price.

Dan Waggoner was one of the North Texas cowmen who learned of the Abilene market in time to trail a herd there in 1867. Other herds headed up the same route from Jack County.[18] Ultimately thirty-five thousand cattle were shipped from Abilene that first season, but because of widespread fears of tick fever, there was little profit to be made in shipping Texas cattle to market until 1868, when they had become popular with meat packers.

News of the cattle market at Abilene spread over the Texas ranges in the fall of 1867, as ranchers prepared herds for the trail in 1868. McCoy sent men to survey the route across Kansas, to shorten it where possible, and to mark it with mounds of earth.

By the spring of 1868 Abilene had been transformed from a sleepy hamlet to a boom town, as men and women flocked there for the pleasure and profit of relieving Texas trail hands of their hard-earned pay. But competitors were already after the Texans' money. Junction City ran ads in Texas newspapers and sent riders to warn trail bosses to avoid sinful Abilene. McCoy countered by sending W. W. Sugg to urge them to take advantage of the facilities and buyers at Abilene. Sugg, who knew many Texas cowmen, was successful, and by mid-April, as several herds approached Abilene, some buyers were already waiting for them.

Cattle continued to arrive, but the buyers had satisfied their needs, and sales ceased. Resourceful as ever, McCoy hired two Spanish California ropers and four Texas cowboys, Mark A. Withers, Jake Carroll, Tom Johnson, and Billy Campbell, and took them and their horses west to the buffalo range. He had cattle cars reinforced and adapted to hold buffalo bulls, wild horses, and elk. Signs on the sides of the cars advertised McCoy's Abilene cattle sales.

McCoy sent the cars to St. Louis, where the cowboys staged roping and riding exhibitions that attracted huge crowds. The cars went next to Chicago, where the performances were equally well attended. While this was going on, McCoy invited Illinois cattle dealers and feeders to accompany him to western Kansas on a buffalo hunt. As a result of these efforts, which cost McCoy six thousand dollars, many more cattle buyers came to Abilene, and all of the cattle were sold, more than seventy-five thousand head for the season. Packers had discovered that the meat of Longhorns was better for packing than that of other breeds, for there was less waste.

Because of widespread losses of cattle in Illinois after Long-horns were brought there for fattening, the state legislature considered a bill prohibiting the importation of Texas cattle. McCoy attended the sessions to lobby against the bill, and finally secured an amendment permitting the entry of stock that had been held over on the plains for the winter. "Wintered" cattle were free of the ticks and no longer spread the deadly fever. It was astonishing, McCoy noted, how many cattle certified as having been wintered appeared at Abilene in the summer of 1869.[19]

In Texas, cattle were always sold by class rather than by weight, and all animals of any class brought the same price regardless of size or condition. A man buying cattle anywhere in Texas paid a fixed price for each yearling, two-year-old, and so forth. But at the railheads buyers bought steers for shipping to market by the pound. Texas cowmen quickly recognized the opportunity to increase their profits by getting their steers to market as fat as possible.

In 1870 more than 300,000 head of Texas cattle were driven to Kansas. Because the railroads east of the Missouri were waging a rate war by lowering shipping charges, some cowmen made profits of between fifteen and twenty-five dollars a head. The result was that in 1871 Kansas was deluged with Texas cattle, for upwards of 600,000 head were trailed north. Heavy rains made the grass poor and the cattle weak. In the meantime the railroads had agreed on high rates for shipping cattle. About half of the cattle were not sold and had to be wintered on the plains. Severe weather, including ice storms, killed an estimated 250,000 head, and many cowmen, including Dan Waggoner, suffered heavy losses.

Although Texas cattlemen had trailed herds to distant markets before the Civil War, the herds were small, and it was only after the Chisholm Trail was opened and traveled by dozens of herds that trail bosses became proficient in handling large numbers of cattle with few men. The first herd up the Chisholm Trail had employed fifty-four cowboys for twenty-four hundred steers, but the large number was partly for protection against plains Indians. Expert trail bosses found that with ten or twelve riders and a cook they could manage a herd of twenty-five hundred head, the optimum size for successful trailing. Under an experienced trail boss and favorable conditions the steers gained weight along the way.

The opening of the Chisholm Trail gave Texas ranchers a large and stable market for their cattle. In the first few years the trail herds were composed largely of "mossy horns" up to ten or twelve years old. As the number of older steers was reduced, trail herds bound for market were mainly beeves, steers that presumably were four years old. Many stock cattle—cows and bulls—were trailed north to the new ranches that spread rapidly as the plains Indians retreated and the buffalo disappeared.

As the plains tribes were gradually confined to reservations, the new Indian agencies added considerably to the demand for Texas cattle, for all of the tribes that had depended on the buffalo had to be fed beef. No state was better prepared to meet this demand than Texas. And when new army posts were garrisoned, the army's requirements also rose. Government contracts provided an important stimulus to cattle raising and the trailing business as long as it lasted.

CHAPTER 2

From Wild Cow Hunts
to Roundups

"The trail life as a whole is easy compared to ranch life."

Duke and Frantz

PUTTING together a herd of ten- or twelve-year-old steers for the trail was difficult and often frustrating work, for mossy horns were hard to catch and troublesome to control. It took expert cowhands, especially Mexican vaqueros, to separate Longhorns from their refuges in the Brasada, or brush country between the Nueces River and the Rio Grande. "Brush popping" was the hardest kind of cow work.

The only horses suitable for brush popping were the little mustangs, or Spanish Texas cow ponies, which enjoyed the chase and were as fearless as the wild cattle. These ponies were cheap, and cowmen considered them expendable; they were often gored and nearly always crippled before their work in the brush was done. Brush popping was a much tougher test of man and horse than handling cattle on the open range. There were, in fact, few similarities between the two types of cow work.

Lee Moore, who in the 1880s was a ranch foreman in Wyoming, recalled conditions in Texas immediately after the Civil War, when recently discharged Confederate soldiers came home to their ranches. Most immediately banded together in small groups to recover lost herds. "We didn't call it roundup in those days," he said. "We called it cow-hunts and every man on this cow-hunt was a cattle owner just home from the war and went out to see what they had left to brand up." Moore, a boy at this time, was looking for his father's cattle.

"We had no wagon," he continued. "Every man carried his grub in a wallet on or behind his saddle and his bed under his saddle." Moore was put on day herding the cattle gathered. "We

Roundup crew and herd in Colorado. Note four-mule chuck wagon, and brand on cow pony on right. The remuda is behind the chuck wagon. Courtesy of the Amon Carter Museum of Western Art, Fort Worth

would corral the cattle every night at some one of the owners' homes and stand guard around the corral."

The men played poker every night for stakes of unbranded cattle. Yearlings were valued at fifty cents a head, and so on up to five dollars for the best beeves. If a man ran out of cattle to wager, he could get back in the game easily; for ten dollars he could buy a stack of twenty yearlings. The cow hunt continued all summer. Every few days each man drove his cattle to his own range, the process later called a throwback.[1]

When a crew was getting ready for a cow hunt in the

Brasada, each man made himself a supply of rawhide hobbles for his cowponies, braided extra rawhide reatas, and repaired any of his equipment in need of it. Every man wore heavy bull-hide leggins, or chaps, a thick brush jacket of leather or Mexican cloth that thorns could not penetrate, a tough hat, and heavy leather gauntlets to protect hands and forearms. The saddles had tapaderos, or leather stirrup coverings, to protect the rider's feet.

When all was ready, they loaded cornmeal and bacon on a pack horse or two, and turned out the decoy herd of tame cattle to use in controlling the wild ones. The only difference between tame and wild cattle was that the tame ones did not high-tail it for distant parts the moment they saw a man on horseback.

Because the range cattle had been neglected during the war years, there was an unusually large number of ten- or twelve-year-old mossy horns among the brush cattle. These were out-laws when it came to being herded by men on horses, and it was necessary to clear them out as quickly as possible, for they made younger cattle more difficult to handle. Mossy horns were as wild as mustangs, and they preserved their freedom with determination. The brush in which they hid was composed of mesquite trees, prickly pears, and a rich variety of other thorny shrubs.

The brush poppers set up camp near a strong corral made by digging a trench about three feet deep and setting up a palisade of ten-foot posts bound at about eye level with strips of rawhide. The corral had wings extending out from both sides of the gate to help keep the cattle from turning back or breaking out.

The cow hunt began when the riders placed the decoy herd in the brush. The moment they entered the brush a mile or two from the decoys, the ponies became especially alert and ready to run, for they could detect the presence of wild cattle before their riders could. When they heard cattle crashing through the brush the eager ponies dashed after them, their riders hanging on and dodging tree limbs and prickly pears as best they could. Some of the ponies threw themselves sideways through the thickets. A rider might be anywhere on his pony except in the saddle; he was paid to hang on, not to maintain his dignity or look graceful, and brush ponies would not stop for anything once the chase began.

Trusting to their ponies' sense of direction, the brush pop-pers tried to run the wild cattle toward the decoys. If all went well, wild and tame cattle were mixed, and the hands quickly surrounded them, loudly singing unmelodious tunes as they rode, presumably to calm the nervous cattle. Slowly and care-fully they eased the herd out of the brush toward the corral near camp. The farther they traveled from the brush the more des-perate the mossy horns were to break away.

Mishaps were frequent, for sometimes wild cattle dashed into the decoy herd so fast there was no stopping them, and the whole bunch left that part of the country. Often, too, on the way to the corral they might lose half of the morning's catch. If a steer broke out and a man went after it, other cattle would race through the gap thus created in the line of riders. Once wild cattle had escaped from a herd they were harder than ever to pen and control. On bad days brush poppers found that by the time they had the herd in the corral there were fewer cattle than they had started with in the morning.

After some brush cattle had been gathered, part of the decoy herd was left with them, and they were closely herded when turned out to graze during the days. In the afternoon the day's catch was brought up and the two herds were thrown together and eased toward the corral. Often they began milling outside the gate, and at such times a few usually escaped. As soon as the gate was closed on the herd, the riders galloped off to rope and tie those that had escaped.

Roping mossy horn outlaws in the brush was the most dangerous part of brush popping, for the ropes had to be tied to saddle horns. A roped bull or steer might dash around one side of a mesquite tree, while the cow pony went the other way. Bull and pony met, often with disastrous results, for a cornered Longhorn was as dangerous as a bear with a sore paw. A powerful mossy horn might break rope or cinch, or turn and charge pony and rider. At such times a rider saved himself by cutting the rope or shooting the Longhorn.

When a cowboy roped a steer in the brush, he tied its head up against a tree. If the decoy herd was near, it was brought up and the steer released into it; usually it went to the center of the herd and stayed there. If the decoy herd was too far, it meant bringing an ox and necking the two together. By passive resistance the ox eventually took the fight out of the steer, and showed up with it hours later at the corral.

Another method of catching outlaw steers was hunting and roping them on moonlight nights when they came out of the brush to graze. At times it was possible to get between the wild cattle and the brush before daybreak, but roping wild cattle was a painfully slow way to build up a herd. Often, however, it was the only way to catch the old mossy horns.

After a small herd had been gathered it was moved to ranch headquarters while the cowboys returned to the brush for more.

Even when moving such herds there was always the likelihood that one of the old outlaws would make a break for freedom. The nearest rider raced after it, and, while riding at full speed, "tailed" or "busted" the steer. Tailing required a fast pony that knew its work, and a skillful, daring rider. As the pony drew alongside the racing steer, the cowboy grabbed its tail and wound it around his saddle horn. The pony put on a burst of speed and turned slightly away, sending the steer flying end over end, perhaps breaking its horns or even its neck. Dazed, it usually trotted meekly back to the herd and gave no more trouble, at least for the rest of the day. As cattle increased in value, such destructive methods were abandoned.

Although Anglo cowmen brought with them from the southern frontier many of the techniques of handling range cattle, tailing was one of the skills they learned from Mexican vaqueros, for whom it was a Sunday sport and popular diversion. A number of vaqueros would round up and pen a bunch of wild bulls. Then amid shouts one bull was let out through the gate, to race over the prairie with a shrieking vaquero in pursuit. He tailed the bull and then rode back to the pen while another took his turn. Injuries occurred, for the swift bulls occasionally turned and charged pony and rider.

Another method of taking the fight out of an outlaw bull or steer was to shoot it through the thick part of its horn. If the bullet struck dead center the shock and pain usually made the animal less pugnacious and more cooperative thereafter. Since such shots were usually made while pony and steer were running at full speed, it was not always possible to hit a horn dead center. If the shot went a bit low and killed the steer no one complained, for cattle were cheap and outlaws were more trouble than they were worth. Cowmen were determined to rid their ranges of troublesome mossy horns, and no one cared if a few were killed in the process.

Brush popping was a special type of cow work for both men and ponies, and its story has never been fully told. Because it was brutally hard on the ponies, three times as many were needed by brush poppers as were required for regular range work. After a day's run the brush ponies were usually full of thorns; many were stiff and lame before they warmed up. The work was equally hard on riders, but brush poppers boasted that they could go anywhere a cow could and stand anything a horse could.

At the end of a day's riding the men pulled thorns from themselves and their ponies. For painful wounds and bruises the remedies were poultices of prickly pear leaves and applications of coal oil or kerosene for both men and horses.

The mossy horns were well known in their own and nearby areas; to "run like a Nueces steer" was a common expression for the most abandoned type of running through or over obstacles. Wild brush cattle had at least one name that was printable— "cactus bloomers."[2]

Cow hunts in the Brasada were dangerous at all times, and not only because of the wild cattle or occasional Comanche raiding parties. The brush country was also the refuge of outlaws, for sheriffs, unless careless of their lives, rarely entered the area in search of wanted men. The Nueces River was the "deadline for sheriffs." Ranchers found it wiser to help fugitives than to arrest them, for it was unhealthful to earn the enmity of men who lived outside the law. As a result of these perils every brush rider was armed, in the early days with cap and ball revolvers known as "outlaws" because when a man pulled the trigger he never knew how many chambers would fire.

Less spectacular denizens of the brush were the lice that swarmed over the men and their clothing. The vaqueros learned from the plains Indians to place their clothes on ant hills until the ants had carried off all of the lice. Then they washed themselves and their clothes with suds made from yucca roots, allowing the suds to dry in order to kill the nits.

Brush poppers lived in isolation from the rest of the world for months at a time, gathering wild cattle for others to drive to the main ranch and put in trail herds. There was no mail, no regular payday. When a man needed clothing or gear or tobacco, it was brought from the main ranch with provisions and charged against his pay. Some vaqueros worked for years without settling their wages, but no wise rancher tried to cheat them. For one thing, it was customary to take a man at his word; for another, cheating a vaquero was a risky way to save a few dollars. Vaqueros were artists with rawhide reatas, and on occasion two mounted men dueled with their reatas until one was caught and dragged to his death.

Brush poppers occasionally got well acquainted with outlaw steers that would not stay captured. In the spring of 1872, for example, a herd of twelve hundred mossy horns was gathered and delivered to a buyer who had come from Kansas with a crew of "shorthorns"—men from farming country. Unaccustomed to handling wild cattle, they reached Kansas with only their saddle horses and work oxen. Some of the wild steers were back in the brush before the next year's cow hunt.

Texans who were accustomed to working in the Brasada often were as reluctant as the cactus bloomers to leave the brush country. One little Texas brush popper tried year after year to accompany a herd up the trail, but each time when they left the wooded regions he fled back to the brush, for the treeless prairies made him nervous.

One spring when he started up the trail as usual, the cowboys hog-tied him and put him in the wagon. They kept him there until he was too far out on the plains to turn back; he stayed with the herd out of fear of leaving it and crossing the plains alone. "You know," he confessed, "when I get out on that big prairie I feel kind of naked."[3]

Mossy horn steers that refused to be driven away from the brush country with trail herds were treated somewhat in the same fashion as the brush popper. After collecting them a second time, when they started up the trail the cowboys necked them to tamer animals. After a few weeks they were herd broken, and had forgotten about turning back.

At first all of the big ranches were near the coast, but bold men began pushing north and west, coming into conflict with the Kiowas and Comanches. One of these was John Simpson Chisum, who in 1854 began ranching in Denton County. He moved his operations in 1862 to the area around the junction of the Colorado and Concho rivers, then in the 1870s moved his cattle to the Bosque Grande on the Pecos in New Mexico.

In 1856 the Reverend George W. Slaughter and his son C.

C. Slaughter settled with their cattle in Palo Pinto County, along with other pioneer families. In times of serious troubles with the Indians, some ranchers sold their cattle for anything they could get and pulled up stakes for safer country. C. C. Slaughter, by buying cattle at such times, became the biggest cowman in this region.

During and after the Civil War, Comanches and Kiowas ran off thousands of Texas cattle to trade to Comancheros from New Mexico. In 1864, for example, they escaped with ten thousand head from Young County, and in the following year drove away two thousand of Charles Goodnight's cattle from the Young-Throckmorton country. These costly raids continued until the mid-1870s, when troops finally defeated the Kiowas and Comanches at Palo Duro Canyon and confined them to their reservations in Indian Territory.

Not all losses were to Indian raiders, for there were also unscrupulous Anglos who stole their neighbors' cattle. Before ranches were fenced, cattle often strayed a hundred miles or more from their home ranges. It was customary, therefore, when a rancher gathered a herd for market, to include all suitable animals regardless of brands. Honest men kept records of these strays and notified their owners. Once a year ranchers held "stock meetings" to settle accounts with the owners of branded strays they had sold, charging only one dollar a head for selling them, a fee owners were quite willing to pay. In 1866 this practice was legalized by the "tallying law" providing for inspectors to make counts of all brands and classes of cattle in trail herds and to record the tallies with county clerks. As long as only honest men were involved, the system was satisfactory, but some men defrauded the owners of cattle they had sold.[4]

There were also cow thieves at work. Many ranchers suffered heavy losses when neighbors sold herds or whole brands. Men buying cattle on range delivery often rounded up all of the cattle regardless of brands and drove them away. Ranchers whose cattle were in such drives, if they learned of it in time, had to follow the herds and cut out the brands that had not been sold, but often they were unaware of their losses until the next roundup. Because of the growing demand for cattle, the Big

Steal persisted. It was not even partially checked until cattlemen formed associations such as the one organized at Graham in 1877.[5] These associations hired inspectors to pursue rustlers and recover stolen cattle, but by that time some cowmen had lost every animal they owned and given up ranching. By the late 1870s cattle were scarce on some Texas ranges.

The old-timers who had clawed out their ranches in the face of Indian raids and cow thieves were convinced that they should enjoy exclusive use of the ranges even if they owned little land. They considered it an infringement of their rights when nesters began plowing up small plots; cowmen looked on the land as having been made for pasture only.

Texas cowmen, according to Joseph McCoy, were prodigal, selfish, and suspicious of "Northern men." They would, he said, stand by their contracts, but not always by their oral agreements, and in his view they were no more courageous than men in general.[6]

"Sanguine and speculative in temperament," McCoy continued, "impulsively generous in free sentiment; warm and cordial in their friendships; hot and hasty in anger; with a strong inate [sic] sense of right and wrong; with a keen sense for the ridiculous and a general intention to do that that is right and honorable in their dealings; they are, as would naturally be supposed, when the manner of their life is considered, a hardy, self-reliant, free and independent class acknowledging no superior or master in the wide universe."[7]

In Texas, despite what McCoy thought, there were few written contracts among old-time cowmen. As one remarked, "I'd rather argue with you a week before a trade than a minute afterwards." Binding contracts were sealed by "It's a trade" and a handshake.[8]

Not all successful Texas cowmen were of masculine gender, for there were also "cattle queens" such as Lizzie Johnson and Mabel Day, who through wisdom and determination made their way on a man's range. Lizzie Johnson earned money to enter the cattle business by teaching in her father's school—the Johnson Institute—near Austin, and by writing and selling articles under a pen name. In 1871 she registered her own brand in Travis

County and expanded her herd in the conventional fashion by having her cowboys mark mavericks with her brand.

When she was thirty-six, Lizzie married Hezekiah Williams, a widowed preacher whose lack of business acumen was undermined further by his fondness for hard liquor. A shrewd businesswoman, Lizzie had no intention of allowing Hezekiah to squander her wealth, so she insisted that their marriage agreement include a contract allowing her to retain both her property and future profits. She and Hezekiah used the same foreman on their ranches, and according to legend she ordered him to put her brand on Hezekiah's unbranded calves. Whether apocryphal or not, this story simply reflects Lizzie's ability to match wits with men and come out a winner.

Lizzie accompanied her own herds up the trail; Hezekiah took his herds at the same time, but these were two independent operations. Lizzie's only concession was to let him share her buggy. She was completely at home with cowmen and, though ever a lady, talked their language. On a number of occasions she saved Hezekiah with substantial loans, but they were dutifully repaid. When he died she bought him an expensive coffin, scrawling across the bill, "I loved this old buzzard this much."[9]

Mabel Day, another Texas cattle queen, inherited her husband's ranch of 77,550 acres in Coleman County, along with upwards of $100,000 in debts. She had to contend with a number of predatory cattlemen, including her late husband's brother and former business associates, who wanted her land and cattle. Hers was a discouraging struggle, but she refused to accept defeat. The courts ignored her protests when the administrator of her husband's estate tried to sell her brother-in-law eighteen hundred yearlings at more than $9,000 below market value. Only after she had posted a bond of $150,000 did the court appoint her executor of the estate. Even then her situation remained precarious.

By negotiating a loan in New York City and a contract with Kentucky bankers and distillers who wanted to buy into the cattle business, she managed to retain her land. At that time the "Fence War" broke out, and miles of her fences were destroyed, an expression of resentment against outsiders investing in Texas cattle ranches. Although she never was able to liquidate all of her debts, her long battle to retain possession of the ranch was successful.[10]

These were but two of the women who were active in the cattle business. There were others, and many ranchers' wives accompanied their husbands up the trail to Kansas. In chapters entitled "Hairpins on the Trail," "Amazons of the Range: The Lady Ranchers," and others, Joyce Gibson Roach has described many women involved in ranching, trailing, and other activities related to the cattle ranges.[11]

As ranching spread out of the brush country to the open plains, the wild cow hunts of the early days became large-scale, cooperative roundups. Each spring the ranchers of a section of the range would agree on a date and a roundup boss. Each of the big outfits sent its crew, remuda, and chuck wagon to the meeting place; small ranchers sent only a man or two. Distant ranchers sent representatives ("reps") to gather their strays. Reps were top hands who knew every brand and earmark of the whole region; they often represented a number of distant ranchers.

While the roundup was on the range of one of the big outfits, the foreman of that ranch was the one who decided where the circle riders would go and where the cattle were to be gathered. He also sent some of his own men, who knew the country, to accompany the circle riders. These men rode their "long horses,"—frequently outlaws with great endurance that couldn't be used for cow work. They swept a large area on the run, driving all of the cattle toward the gathering ground at the center of the circle. Riding hard, the circle riders might cover forty miles before all of the cattle were on the gathering ground.

After lunch and a change of horses, the men sorted, or cut, the cattle, separating them by brands. The local rancher was the first to cut out his cattle from the herd, which might number five thousand head. It was here that the top riders on cutting horses moved quietly into the herd and separated the cows and calves according to brands.

When this was finished, the branding began. The best ropers skillfully tossed loops on the calves and dragged them to the

Branding calves on an Oklahoma ranch in 1888. Not shown are the ropers and fires for heating branding irons. Wrestling calves at branding time was hard work. Courtesy of the Oklahoma Historical Society

fire, calling out the brands of the cows so the calves could be correctly marked. Flankers grabbed the calves and held them down; one man did the branding while another cut the owner's earmark and castrated the bull calves. Every tenth bull calf was left intact to serve as a range bull; no effort was made to choose the best animals for herd sires.

At first the mavericks belonged to the ranch that claimed the range. Later the cattle raisers' associations sold the mavericks at auction, using the funds to aid cattlemen.

After the branding was completed, the herds from other ranges were moved along to the next gathering ground. Every few days men came to drive them back to their own ranges, the process called a "throwback." In the meantime, the herds had to be kept under control day and night to prevent them from straying or mixing with others. This meant that the cowboys rode hard all morning, wrestled calves in the heat and dust all

Cowboys castrating a bull calf, Judith River roundup, 1910. Courtesy of
Keith Anderson, Helena, Montana

afternoon, and then took a turn at night herding. Depending on how large an area the roundup covered, they might be out with a wagon for several months at a time.

The spring gathering was the calf roundup, for it was primarily to brand the new calves. The beef roundup in the fall was for the purpose of separating steers that were old enough to market, but it was also a time for branding late calves or any that had been missed in the spring.

When the big ranches were fenced with barbed wire in the late 1870s and 1880s, the old-time cooperative roundup was no longer necessary, for cattle could not stray from their own ranges. It was also possible, once pastures were securely fenced, to control breeding and begin upgrading herds. Many ranchers bought Shorthorn or Hereford bulls, for these cattle reached maximum weight much sooner than Longhorns.

The coming of barbed wire also meant that ranchers had to acquire title to rangeland, for it was no longer possible to own merely enough land for ranch house and corrals and to control strategic water sources. Old-timers who had grown up in the era of free grass and open range refused to accept this unwanted change without a struggle; one called barbed wire the curse of West Texas. Although the use of barbed wire in Texas began in 1876, most free grass men didn't feel the pinch until the summer drought of 1883. When they found access to grass and water elsewhere cut off, they realized for the first time the full impact that barbed wire was having on their way of life. The "Fence War" began as free grass men cut down mile after mile of barbed wire fences. As the conflict became more intense through central Texas, the governor called a special session of the legislature, which made fence-cutting a felony as of January 1884. In the meantime, cattle thieves had taken advantage of the opportunity to strip some ranches of cattle and horses.

After the rain, in the rope corral. Horses were trained to respect the rope corral on the trail. In the background is the hoodlum wagon loaded with bedrolls; the team is harnessed, ready to be hitched. Photo by L. A. Huffman. Courtesy of the Amon Carter Museum of Western Art, Fort Worth

CHAPTER 3

Life on the Trail

"This procession of countless cattle on their
slow march to the north was one of the most
interesting and distinctive features of the
West."

Richard Harding Davis

WHEN the Chisholm Trail opened the way to an expanding market, Texas cowmen welcomed the opportunity to sell their surplus cattle. Most of the men who took part in the early drives knew little about what to expect north of the Red River. For trail bosses and cowboys alike, the only place to learn trailing techniques was on the trail.

A man who planned to put together a herd in the spring began his preparations in the fall by visiting ranchers and arranging with each for the delivery of a certain number of beeves to a fenced pasture at a specified date. The drover acquired a chuck wagon, engaged a cook, bought horses for the remuda, then hired the experienced cowboys who were available and enough youths to make up a crew.

Cook and crew assembled before the ranchers began delivering their cattle. Some or most of the horses might be half-wild and unbroken, and the cowboys went to work on them. Each man, starting with the boss, chose his string of mounts; from it he selected the most reliable animal for his night horse. The remuda had to be trained to stay in the rope corral used on the trail as a catch pen. It was simply several lariats tied together and attached to trees or chuck wagon wheels, and was only the symbol of a corral. But when a horse broke out, a cowboy roped and "busted" him hard. By the time the herd was ready, every horse in the remuda respected the rope corral.

As each rancher brought in his beeves the boss cut out and rejected any considered unsatisfactory. He counted the others

33

into the pasture, making a tally of the various brands, so owners of strays could be reimbursed after the cattle were sold. When the herd had been gathered, the trail crew spent the next few days putting a road brand on them, to identify any that might stray. The road brand also enabled inspectors to check trail herds for cattle being moved illegally. Road branding was a Spanish practice adopted unofficially at first; in 1871 a law required that all cattle being moved out of the state must bear road brands that were large and easily identified. In the early days the cattle had to be roped and thrown; later long chutes were built so that fifteen or twenty could be branded at one time, speeding up the process and reducing the danger of injuries to men and animals.

When all was ready, they shaped up the herd, opened the pasture gate, and headed north, accompanied at first by extra hands. For several days they pushed the cattle fairly hard to get them away from their customary ranges and to make them too tired to run at night. After about a week the cattle usually settled down and were considered trail broken. Then the extra hands took their bedrolls and headed home.

Once across the Red River the herd was in Indian Territory, and in the late 1860s and early 1870s the danger of Indian attack made all hands apprehensive. In 1867 the Kiowas, Comanches, Southern Cheyennes, and Arapahoes had been persuaded to accept the Treaty of Medicine Lodge Creek, in which they gave up the right to roam and presumably accepted the concept of confinement on reservations. Some of the warriors of these tribes, however, preferred to die fighting instead of starving to death on the reservations. When they came upon a herd they might simply demand a few cattle, or they might attack the cowboys and stampede the cattle and horses.

Indians weren't the only hazard to early trail herds, for buffaloes and mustangs might charge through the line of cattle, scattering them beyond recovery. Trail bosses hired "buffalo whoopers" to ride ahead of the cattle each day and frighten away any herds of buffalo or mustangs that were close enough to the trail to cause trouble.

By the time a herd reached Indian Territory its travel was

Crew bedding down for the night by the hoodlum wagon. Cowboy removing boots still has hat on. The hat was the first item of clothing put on in the morning and the last to be removed at night. Photo by F. M. Steel. Courtesy of the Amon Carter Museum of Western Art, Fort Worth

usually routine, and the cattle moved along by habit. The strongest steers had taken their place as leaders; others had positioned themselves somewhere in the long column, and they took approximately the same place each day. At the rear were the drags, the weak and sore-footed cattle whose protection and safe delivery were vital to the success of the drive.

The greenest men were assigned to the drags, for good hands wouldn't accept the distasteful, dirty, menial task because of the constant dust. Drag riders came away from the herd each evening with a heavy coating of dust on their hats and dust as "thick as fur" on their eyebrows and mustaches. Flankers and swing men on the side away from the wind were not much better off. The thousands of cattle pulverized the ground into fine dust, "and looking at a herd being driven at a distance one could only see a great cloud of dust rising to the heavens."[1]

A typical day began with the last change of guards before breakfast at three-thirty or four o'clock in the morning. Those heading for their blankets for half an hour more of precious sleep awakened the cook, who stirred up his fire and started breakfast. The rattle of pots and pans told the wrangler it was time to ride out and look for the remuda. When breakfast was nearly ready, the boss and the pointers arose so they could eat and be with the herd when it drifted from the bed ground. The cook called the men, who arose, put on their hats, then struggled to get their feet into damp, tight-fitting boots, hopping around on one foot and filling the air with profanity. Next they tied up their bedrolls and threw them beside the wagon. By the time the men had finished breakfast the wrangler was ready to push the horses into the rope corral.

There were no pets among the horses, and not one of them would allow a man to walk up and tie a rope around its neck; range horses that were easy to catch were easily stolen. On roundup or the trail the usual practice was for one or two of the best ropers to do all of the corral roping. Since not all cowboys were expert ropers it saved time and was easier on the horses for cowboys to hand their lariats to the roper and call out the names of the horses they wanted.

By the time the boss and pointers reached the herd the cattle were beginning to leave the bed ground and graze, always toward the north. The pointers positioned themselves well back from the lead steers so the cattle could spread out and graze along at their own pace. The boss loped ahead to decide on watering places for the day and a suitable place to rest the herd at noon.

As the herd moved slowly away from the bed ground the riders eased into position around it. Pointers and drag riders resumed the same place each day, but swing and flank men rotated. As the herd grazed along for several hours all the men had to contend with was boredom, for usually there was little to occupy them unless the boss signaled a change of direction.

When the cattle had eaten their fill they began walking steadily along the trail, stretching out into a long line.

At noon the boss signaled to push the herd off the trail; no other order was necessary, for the men knew exactly what to do. Half of the crew—left point man, right swing, left flanker, and right drag rider—headed for the wagon. They ate quickly, saddled fresh horses from the remuda, and loped back to the herd. To a hungry man with the herd there was no more welcome sight than his relief coming at a good clip.[2]

At supper time the riders again came in shifts to eat. If there was no nighthawk to herd the remuda, every man hobbled his own string except for his night horse, which he saddled and picketed near where he threw his bedroll. Because of the widespread belief that white horses attracted lightning in the dark, they were shunned as night horses. At least one episode suggests that there may have been some foundation for this belief about white animals and lightning. In 1854 a herd bound for California was struck by a violent thunderstorm in southwestern New Mexico. A bolt of lightning struck a white steer, then leaped to another white one fifty yards away, killing both.[3]

When the herd was bedded down for the night, about nine o'clock, all but the first or cocktail guard headed for the wagon. At times the men sat around the wagon for a time talking or listening to some cowboy fiddler playing "Billy in the Low Ground," "Dinah Had a Wooden Leg," "Hell among the Yearlin's," or other favorites of the day. Much of the talk was about the stars.[4]

Cowboys knew the major stars and planets from nights on guard around a herd, and had their own names for them. They learned to tell time by the rising or setting of certain stars or constellations with surprising accuracy. The Big Dipper, which Mexicans called *el reloj de los Yaquis*—the Yaquis' watch—was the principal cowboy timepiece. The men of the last guard agreed, however, that the Morning Star was the most beautiful sight in the sky, for its rising meant that the cook was starting breakfast and the wrangler was riding out after the remuda.[5]

Night herding was one of the daily trials of the cattle drive, although when the weather was pleasant and the cattle were quiet, it meant only the loss of two hours of sleep. Lack of sleep was, in fact, the most persistent complaint on the trail, for even under the most favorable conditions there was never time for a full night's sleep for any man. When conditions were bad, the men might go without sleep for forty-eight hours. At such times some kept themselves awake by rubbing tobacco juice in their eyes. As one trail boss said, "If you expect to follow the trail, son, you must learn to do your sleeping in the winter."[6]

The men who had to night herd from midnight to two in the morning had about three hours' sleep, then about an hour and a half more when they came off guard. But if the crew got one hour of sleep or none it made no difference, for in the morning the wagon and the herd moved on. If all hands were in the saddle all night following a stampeding herd or one drifting before a norther, at daybreak they ate breakfast, saddled fresh horses, and went back to the cattle to start another day's work.

Night herding got to be as much a part of a cowboy's life as anything else on the trail. The men had the same hours every night and by habit awakened when their turn came. Usually a sleeping man could hear the hoofbeats of the night guard's horse trotting toward the wagon. He would climb out of his blankets, pull on hat and boots, gulp down a cup of coffee, and untie his night horse. After one herd had reached the Mussel-shell River in Montana, the boss decided night herding was un-necessary. Every man woke up when it was his turn to go on guard, wondering what was wrong.[7]

It was at night that electrical storms caused much trouble. Anything, on occasion, could set off a stampede, but thunder and lightning started more runs from bed grounds than any-thing else. Signs that trouble was coming were often detected in the nervousness of the cattle, but many a rider's first warning came from the actions of his night horse, which always alerted him to any dangers it sensed.

Far in the distance a line of dark clouds might appear near the horizon, clouds that were eerily lighted by flashes of light-ning so far away the men could barely hear the thunder. The air would turn deathly still and humid; sweat poured down the riders' faces and stung their eyes. Gradually the flashes became brighter and the rolls of thunder grew louder. A heavy mist rose from the ground, so that the riders strained their eyes to see their ponies' ears, for these relayed warning signals. Balls of electricity—Saint Elmo's fire—played around the tips of the horses' ears and the steers' horns, leaping snakelike from tip to tip around the herd, while the riders held their breath and hoped they had left everything metallic in the wagon. Deliberately, as if controlled by malevolent spirits, the blackest clouds poised menacingly over the herd.

A blinding flash of lightning lighted up the countryside; then all was plunged into total blackness. By the time the deafening thunderclap had ended, the rumble of hoofs and clatter of horns rose above the roar of the storm. Longhorns did not rise to their feet and then stampede—it was "one jump to their feet and running and the next jump to hell." As Charlie Russell said, "The confidence a steer's got in the dark is mighty frail."[8]

Blinded by the lightning, the cowboys could only loosen their reins, strangle their saddle horns, and hope their ponies did not fall over a bluff. Running cattle invariably turned gradually to the right. The night ponies, wise to the way of Longhorns, edged forward on the dead run along the left side of the herd to press the leaders into turning, to make a mill or pinwheel. If the cattle were spread out on a wide front there was no hope of starting them milling, but if they were strung out in a line the leaders could be turned and the others would follow. Once the cattle were milling they stopped running; when they were quiet the cowboys unpeeled the mill much as they had started it, and again tried to settle the cattle down for the night. They never returned to the original bed ground, for that would invite another stampede.

Some storms moved off quickly, before the cattle had run far or scattered badly. Others seemed strangely attached to the cattle, and herd and storm roared along together for miles. On such occasions the weary riders and their ponies simply hung on. Every time there was a flash of lightning over the herd a

A cowboy's funeral, one of the few times cowboys were bareheaded.
The Montana Historical Society

momentary silence followed as all the cattle leaped into the air at
the same time. When they hit the ground together the earth
trembled.

Under these circumstances all the riders could do was to
follow bunches of cattle that turned off to one side or the other
and hold them together till morning. When the sun finally rose,
the men with small bunches of cattle drove them toward the
wagon, or in what they thought was the right direction. They
pushed the cattle onto the highest ground so they could look for
other riders.

Gradually the herd was reassembled and strung out to be
counted. When they knew how many were missing, riders
combed the country for miles around looking for strays. If
fortunate, they might recover all but a few that were killed or
maimed in the flight. But if the cattle had run all night, several
hundred might never be found.

After one stampede Teddy Blue Abbott helped bury a cowboy whose horse had fallen in front of the cattle. Not knowing that a man had fallen, the other cowboys had milled the cattle at that place until morning. After that episode the men were ordered to sing or yell when running with a stampede, so others could tell where they were. But cattle would not run over a man if they could avoid it; more men were killed by lightning than by stampeding cattle.[9]

At a particular time when the cattle were ready to run, almost anything could start a stampede. One was caused by a steer getting his hoof caught in an empty tomato can. Another time a night guard's horse got his hoof caught in the tree of a McClellan saddle. One herd was passing Camp Verde when the remuda, frightened by the army's camels, stampeded and scattered the cattle so badly that it took days to find them. On another occasion Jim M. Dobie had made the first day's drive with a herd and penned it in a pasture so the trail crew could have a good night's sleep. Before anyone got to sleep a peacock screeched and the cattle were gone. As a result no one slept.[10]

As Charlie Russell noted, stampedes were noisy, but any harm they caused was usually to the cattle. The losses might range from a few steers crippled to the loss of the entire herd. The extreme disaster occurred to a herd of two thousand steers belonging to Wilson Brothers. When the steers were west of the Brazos, an electrical storm started them running, and the whole herd plunged into "Stampede Gully." Every animal was lost.

Rainstorms might blanket the trail for days, turning the prairie into a miserable bog and making the grass poor so the ponies grew weak and the cattle lost weight. Cooks were hard pressed to prepare hot food, and the men were soaked to the skin and cold for days at a time. No one slept in a dry bed. When relieved from duty with the herd, three exhausted men would lie down in a triangle, each resting his head on another's ankles to keep his face out of the water.

One trail crew driving a herd of yearlings north was struck at night by a blue norther near a dry lake bed that was covered with large tumbleweeds. Soon the tumbleweeds were flying among the bleating yearlings, which scattered in all directions. In the dark it was impossible to tell yearlings from tumbleweeds, and one cowboy chased a bunch of weeds for half a mile trying to force the leaders to turn.[11]

At times storms struck when several herds were in the same area, perhaps waiting for a swollen river to subside. When that happened ten thousand cattle from four or five herds might be so badly mixed it took a week to separate them. Usually there was not enough time to complete the job down to the last steer, and each boss had to rely on the others to keep track of the cattle they sold and reimburse the owners.

Even when the cattle did not stampede, electrical storms could be terrifying, and they sometimes killed men and animals. In 1885 young John Conner was nighthawk of a remuda on the Salt Fork of the Red River when a severe thunderstorm struck. As the air became charged with electricity the horses crowded around him, heads between their front legs and moaning loudly. More terrified than the horses, Conner slid to the ground and lay flat until the storm passed.

During thunderstorms cowboys often prayed loudly, making all sorts of promises, then laughed about them in the morn-

ing. In one violent hailstorm on the North Platte, however, old
Matt Winter lost his temper. Shaking his fist skyward, he
shouted, "All right, you old bald-headed bastard son of a bitch
up there, if you want to kill me come on and do it!" The other
cowboys fearfully begged him to stop.[12]

After a brutal thunderstorm near the Platte the men with an
Olive herd were in the saddle several days rounding up the
scattered cattle, stopping only long enough to eat and saddle
fresh horses. When the herd was finally gathered, one weary
cowboy said to Teddy Blue Abbott, "Teddy I am going to
Greenland where the nights are six months long, and I ain't
going to get up until ten o'clock the next day." "What the hell are
you kicking about?" the boss asked. "You can sleep all winter
when we get to Montana."[13]

After trailing became fairly routine, trail bosses or cowboys
often put a fast horse in the remuda, not for use on the trail but
for racing against others when a number of herds were close
together or at some trail town. Cowboys bet heavily on their
favorites. In the spring of 1877 young Jesse James Benton
joined Tobe Odem's big herd of beeves from Goliad. Benton,
whose family had recently moved from Kentucky, took along the
small Thoroughbred mare, Gray Eagle, that his father had given
him when he thought she wouldn't amount to much because of
her size. But Gray Eagle proved to be exceptionally fast for short
races, defeating many larger Quarter Horses.

There were other herds on the trail, and Odem, after
satisfying himself as to the mare's speed, matched her against a
big buckskin from another remuda, a horse that had won many
races. The bet was for half interest in a bunch of "pick up"
steers, or strays. Cowboys from all of the herds in the vicinity
came to watch and wager; Odem confidently bet five hundred
dollars in cash as well as the cattle. Because the buckskin was
large and well known, most of the cowboys bet on him, but they
were disappointed, for Gray Eagle easily beat him. Odem, who
won nearly four hundred steers as well as considerable cash,
gave Benton fifty dollars of his winnings.[14]

Horse racing was not the only excitement for Odem's men
that trip. Near Dodge City six well-dressed women came out to
the herd in a coach to visit Odem. The cowboys gave them all

nicknames; one who was over six feet tall they called "Latigo Liz." The women stayed several days, insisting that they must see a stampede.

On the second afternoon Odem told them, "There's a bad storm coming and they will sure run tonight." He assigned each lady a dependable night horse and a cowboy for a partner, to keep her out of danger. The storm struck and the steers ran; drenched and with hair flying, the ladies had a great time.

In the morning "an old mutton-head cowboy" told Latigo Liz that she didn't need to be afraid of cattle or buffalo running over her.

"Why?" she asked.

"Because you could just jerk up your dress and stand on one leg and they would think you had clumb a tree, and pass you by."

Latigo Liz laughed. "I do not doubt it at all," she said. Jeff, the Negro cook, was horrified at the old cowboy's remarks, and chided him for his bad manners.[15]

Before the stocking of the northern ranges generated a steady demand for Texas horses as well as cattle, after a herd was sold in Kansas the cowboys, accompanied by the cook and chuck wagon, drove the remuda and perhaps a lead steer back to the home range. On these trips they amused themselves by roping buffalo, hunting, or fishing.

Later, remudas were sold along with the cattle heading for Wyoming or Montana, except for one horse apiece for the men. Eventually all of the horses were sold, and the men were given "cowboy tickets" to Texas on one of the railroads. The first trips by rail were usually entertaining for the passengers, for the cowboys ducked whenever the train went across a bridge or under a trestle. One night some cowboys were asleep on a train that had stopped on a siding to let another pass. When the other train came roaring and whistling past it frightened the cowboys out of their wits. They ran down the aisle, with "Dog Face" Smith in the lead. "Stampede!" one shouted. "Circle your leaders and keep up the drags!"[16]

Conditions on the trail were much improved in the 1880s over those of the previous decade. The chuck wagon was fully developed, and since it was drawn by a four-mule team it was able to carry a wider variety of foods. Saddles, too, were greatly improved, so that sore-backed horses, common on earlier drives, were now rare.[17]

At the outset of the trailing era, the men had used any type of saddle available and wore whatever clothing they might possess, often remnants of Confederate uniforms. They looked, Jesse Benton noted, "like a bunch of cotton-pickers." New styles gradually developed as certain items of clothing or equipment proved their durability and usefulness on the long drive. In 1867 the prevailing saddle style had narrow stirrups and long tapaderos. Riders rested their weight on their toes when they stood in their stirrups. Saddle trees varied widely, but the favorite had a broad horn pointing upward at a forty-five-degree angle. Bridles were functional rather than ornamental, made from rawhide rubbed and grained until reasonably soft and pliable. A few men wove horsehair bridles or bought them from vaqueros. There were also bridles of braided rawhide, and the best lariats were of the same material.

Homespun clothing was protected against hard and constant usage by adding leather caps at the knees and leather seats. Some men made leggins (chaps) of calfskin, hair side out, or of tanned buckskin fringed down the outsides.[18]

By 1872 everything had changed to some degree, especially styles of equipment. Broad stirrups, invented by an old fellow who ranched along the Llano River, had become popular because they were easier on the feet. Riders now shortened their stirrup leathers so that their knees were bent when their feet were in the stirrups. Saddles had broad, flat horns and were higher in front than in the back; most of them also had saddle pockets of goat or bear skin. Spurs with long shanks had replaced those with little straight shanks and sharp rowels. Cowboys now also wore buckskin gloves.[19]

One of the earliest saddles made in Anglo Texas was the little apple horn from Corpus Christi, which was widely used in the 1870s and 1880s even though its tree often caused sores on the horses' backs. Another saddle soon available was made in Fort Worth by Padgett. It was an improvement over the apple horn, but it also contained flaws in design. Still others were

An old-time Texas cowboy on a twenty-dollar pony and forty-dollar saddle, San Antonio, 1880. He has tapaderos on his stirrups and rawhide lariat on his saddle. Western History Collections, University of Oklahoma Library.

produced by Frazier and by Dunn Brothers, Andrews, and Alexander of San Angelo, Texas, and by Gallup in Pueblo, Colorado. For a time one of the most famous saddles was made by H. H. Heiser of Denver.[20]

The California saddle, long used by Mexicans of that region, became popular among cowboys all over the West, for it was comfortable for both horse and rider. The merits of the California saddle, according to Randolph Marcy,

> consist in its being light, strong, and compact, and conforming well to the shape of the horse. When strapped on, it rests so firmly in position that the strongest pull of a horse upon a lariat attached to the pommel can not displace it. Its shape is such that the rider is compelled to sit nearly erect, with his legs on the continuation of the line of the body, which makes his seat more secure. . . . His position is attained by setting the stirrup-leathers farther back than on the old-fashioned saddle. The pommel is high, like the Mexican saddle. . . . The tree is covered with raw hide, put on green and sewed; when this dries it contracts and gives it great strength. It has no iron in its composition, but is kept together by buckskin strings, and can easily be taken to pieces for mending or cleaning. It has a hair girth about five inches wide.

> The whole saddle is covered with a large and thick sheet of sole leather, having a hole to lay over the pommel; it extends back over the horse's hips, and protects them from rain, and when taken off in camp furnishes a good security against dampness when placed under the traveler's bed.

> The California saddle-tree is regarded by many as the best of all others for the horse's back, and as having an easier seat than the Mexican.[21]

Texans always used double-rigged or rim-fire saddles because they tied their lariats to the saddle horns, and the extra cinch was needed when they roped bulls or heavy steers. Dally ropers, who wound the lariat around the saddle horn and could let out slack if necessary, preferred the single-rigged or center-fire California saddles. The saddle came to be a cowboy's most prized possession. "He sold his saddle" meant that a man was down and out, finished, disgraced. He "hung up his saddle" when he was too old to ride; when he "sacked his saddle," it was time for his funeral.[22]

The old saddles had long seats and no swell, which made it difficult for riders to stay on bucking horses. Cowboys often rolled up their slickers or blankets and tied them across the front of the saddle, thereby creating a swell, or "buckin' roll," that aided them in staying on bucking horses. In the 1890s some saddle makers introduced swelled forks like those of modern bronc saddles. The first one, called the "Ellensburg," was made in 1892 by the T. M. Farrell shop in Ellensburg, Washington. Cowboys everywhere at first made fun of the swell-fork saddles, but men who rode the "rough strings" soon appreciated the advantages.[23]

At first saddles were purchased from local shops, but soon they were available from mail-order houses. Catalogs and order blanks from the Garcia Saddle Company of Elko, Nevada, or the Visalia Saddle Company of Visalia, California, or similar ones in Denver and elsewhere were placed in bunkhouses all over the cattle kingdom. The Justin Boot Company, at the suggestion of rancher O. C. Cato, designed a self-measuring method of determining boot sizes. Thereafter boots could also be ordered ready-made.[24]

Before good manila hemp ropes were available, braided rawhide lariats were most widely used, though some men used cotton, sea grass, or Mexican maguey ropes. None was serviceable under all conditions. After sea grass ropes became plentiful, they replaced both rawhide hobbles and reatas.

Except for Bull Durham roll-your-own cigarettes and high-heeled boots, which remained virtually unchanged for more than half a century, most clothing and equipment changed from time to time. Slickers and tarpaulins came into use and were of great service in keeping the men and their bedding dry. Both were made of strong cotton cloth so thoroughly saturated with linseed oil that they readily turned water. Tanned leather replaced rawhide in bridles, and instead of simple split-ear headstalls they had brow and nose bands, throat latches, chin straps, and roller bits.

In the early 1870s wide-brimmed black or brown low-crowned beaver hats were popular, replacing sombreros for a time before they were also superseded by Stetson hats, introduced in the 1870s. In the 1870s, too, the heavy denim riveted pants made by the Levi Strauss Company of San Francisco, and Justin boots made in Texas, both began playing their key role in cowboy clothing. Before the coming of Levis the striped or checkered woolen "California" pants made in Oregon City had been considered the best for riding. "Justins," "Levis," and "Stetsons" became synonymous with boots, pants, and hats in much of the West.

By the 1880s regional styles had developed in clothing, riding gear, and ways of handling horses and cattle. A glance at a strange rider was usually enough to determine where he was from. Montana cowboys, for example, wore narrow-brimmed, low-crowned Stetsons creased with four dents, never with a leather or horsehair hat band. They also customarily wore vests. In the winter Montana cowboys wore the heavy wool California pants with buckskin sewed over the seat and down the insides of the legs. They also wore heavy Angora chaps of white, black, burnt orange, or red colors.[25]

Texans, whether on their home ranges or on those the Matador and other big outfits leased in Montana, wore high-crowned, wide-brimmed hats with creases down the middle and no dents. Most still tucked their pants in their boots. They wore leather shotgun chaps with fringes, or bat-wing chaps.

The Texans also used their small mustang cow ponies or larger Quarter Horse and mustang crosses. The Montana cowpunchers (this term was rarely used in Texas) rode larger, longer-legged, and heavier horses that were strong enough to battle snowdrifts in the winter.[26]

Once the herd reached the end of the trail and the hands were paid and allowed to go into town, they were more eager to catch up on entertainment than on sleep. First they visited a barbershop and had their shaggy manes trimmed. Then they bought a new outfit of clothing from the skin out, bathed, dressed, and headed for the nearest saloon, dance hall, or gambling house.

In releasing their pent-up feelings young cowboys were

boisterous and noisy, and if they could not make loud enough sounds with their vocal cords they made up for it by firing their pistols. The dance halls in the cattle towns along or at the end of the trail were their favorite haunts. Men were obliged to buy drinks for their partners between dances, and one might surmise that the dancers became increasingly carefree as the night wore on. Joseph McCoy commented that "few more wild, reckless scenes of abandoned debauchery can be seen on the civilized earth, than a dance house in full blast in one of the many frontier towns. To say they dance wildly or in an abandoned manner is putting it mild."[27]

When new ranches were opened on the northern plains, many Texas cowboys stayed on with the cattle and remained thereafter in Wyoming or Montana. Others headed for Texas by horse or by train, vowing never again to take part in a long drive. But when spring came and trail bosses were signing up crews, the vows were often forgotten. As Ben Borroum of Del Rio expressed it, "Like many others, when I had work for the time being I did not think I would ever make another trip up the trail, but also like many others, when the next drive came I was 'rarin' to go."[28] There was a fascination about going up the trail that young cowboys found impossible to resist.

CHAPTER 4

The Trail Boss

"The trail drives produced a man unlike any
other that had as yet appeared in the West."
Clifford Westermeier

THE trail boss was the key man in a successful cattle drive, for he
bore the whole responsibility for getting the herd safely to its
destination in good condition. Jim Flood, Andy Adams's semi-
fictional trail boss, explained their duties to his cowboys before
they started up the trail.

"Boys," he said,

the secret of trailing cattle is never to let your herd know
that they are under restraint. Let everything that is done be
done voluntarily by the cattle. From the moment you let
them off the bedground in the morning until they are bedded at night, never let a cow take a step, except in the
direction of its destination. In this manner you can loaf
away the day, and cover from fifteen to twenty miles, and
the herd in the meantime will enjoy all the freedom of an
open range. Of course, it's long, tiresome hours to the men;
but the condition of the herd and saddle stock demands
sacrifices on our part, if any have to be made. And I want to
caution you younger boys about your horses; there is such a
thing as having ten horses in your string, and at the same
time being afoot. You are all well mounted, and on the
condition of the *remuda* depends the success and safety of
the herd. Accidents will happen to horses, but don't let it be
your fault; keep your saddle blankets dry and clean, for no
better word can be spoken of a man than that he is careful
of his horses. Ordinarily a man might get along with six or
eight horses, but in such emergencies as we are all liable to
meet, we have not a horse to spare, and a man afoot is
useless.[1]

51

Andy Adams, whose books on trailing cattle were based on experience. *The Log of a Cowboy* and *The Outlet* are regarded as the most authentic accounts of life on the trail. Courtesy of the Amon Carter Museum of Western Art, Fort Worth

It is unlikely that any trail boss ever stated the requirements more clearly or succinctly than Flood. It often happened, before successful trailing practices became well known, that riders used up their horses and were practically afoot before the drive ended. "Watch out for the cows' hoofs and the horses' backs" was the first rule of trail bosses.

Managing a trail herd required knowledge gained only by experience with cattle, horses, and men as well as acquaintance with the country, the rivers, and the weather. The good trail boss was a man of stoic patience and endurance who was also cautious, alert, and fearless. He might drive himself and his men, but he pushed the cattle only on the rare occasions when it was necessary to cover long distances between watering places.

At the outset the trail boss had to select his crew for the drive, and this required the ability to size up men so as to pass over any of doubtful quality. On the trail tension was often high for days, and men who were likely to break down, become quarrelsome, or panic in emergencies were poor risks. Since only about one-third of the trail hands made the trip more than once, most crews included men who were inexperienced in trailing cattle. At times when dozens of herds were going up the trail, bosses often had to search widely to find enough men.

When young cowboy James Henry Cook asked trail boss Joel Roberts for a job with his herd, Roberts looked him over and said, "Now if you can ride the next four months without a whole night's sleep, and turn your gun loose on any damned Injun that tries to get our horses, well get ready."[2]

On the trail the boss and point riders ate before the others, while the herd began drifting from the bed ground. The boss rode ahead to check on grass and water and to choose the bed ground for the night. He was in the saddle as long as any man with the drive, and might ride thirty or forty miles each day while the herd traveled twelve or fifteen. Because of the need to find good grass and water, herds seldom traveled in a straight line to the north.

After he had scouted ahead, the trail boss might appear on a hill a mile from the herd, where he employed signaling techniques similar to those of the plains Indians. A motion of his hat meant for the men to move the herd out. The pointers repeated it to the swing men, who passed it along to the flankers, who relayed it to the drag riders bringing up the rear.

If the streams ahead had dried up and water was scarce, the boss returned to the herd and told the men to move the cattle faster. This meant that flank and swing and drag riders rode closer to the cattle, causing them to walk faster and graze less. The boss saddled a fresh horse from his string and galloped off to search for water. When he had found an adequate stream, directly ahead or to either side, he rode back to a hill from which he could see the herd, then signaled to the pointers which direction to take.

To signal a change of direction the trail boss galloped his horse in the direction to follow, then signaled with his hat to come along. Again the point men relayed the signal down the line to the drags. If the turn was to the right, the point, flankers, and swing men on that side dropped back and away from the cattle. The men on the left pressed the steers, forcing them to turn, with the result that the whole herd swung in the desired direction at the same time. If the swing men and flankers performed their job skillfully, the sore-footed drag cattle were spared about three hundred yards of walking. Making it easier on the weaker cattle was one of the signs of good trail management. The drags determined the speed of the herd; the stronger cattle often had to be held back so that gaps did not occur in the line. Whenever there were gaps the cattle trotted to catch up with those ahead, and running cattle lost weight. One of the drag riders' jobs was "keeping up the corners" to prevent the rear cattle from spreading out more widely than the swing cattle in front of them, to avoid danger of losses from overheating. The heat generated by a herd was surprising even when it moved slowly, but especially during stampedes.

The trail boss also checked on the horses frequently, to see if any were missing. Experienced men could glance at a remuda of a hundred horses and know when two or three were not there. Most could also name the ones that were absent.

Grazing and watering were daily necessities that must be

accomplished perfectly if the herd was to arrive in good condition. When there were many herds on the trail, finding good grass became critical for the trail boss. Cattle bedded down at night without having had their fill of grass and water were likely to stampede, and running cattle might be lost or crippled. At intervals along the way the cattle were strung out and counted. This was, of course, always done after a stampede or any difficulty in which some cattle might have been separated from the herd.

Veteran trail bosses like Jim Dobie and Ab Blocker learned that the most effective way to control a stampede was to leave all of the men but one or two experienced cowboys at the wagon. Two or three men were usually able to calm the cattle more quickly than a lot of yelling cowboys.

Watering a trail herd was an orderly process. First the cook watered his team and filled the barrel, then the remuda was watered. Next came the cattle; when they had finished drinking, the trail crew had its turn. "I ain't kickin'," one remarked, "but I had to chew that water before I could swaller it." One of the highest compliments that could be paid a trail boss was that he was skillful in watering a herd. J. A. Smiley commented that Henry Eubanks of the XIT was "a real cowman and the best trail man I ever saw. He could water more cattle in a small lake of water and never get it muddy than any man I ever saw."[3]

Burgess and Harry Rutter watered two thousand head at a spring that was about as big as a wagon box, according to Teddy Blue Abbott. If the big beeves had been allowed to crowd in, they would have made a mud hole out of it. The two men brought them up in little bunches and watered a few at a time. "It was," Abbott concluded, "the slickest piece of cow work I ever saw in my life."[4]

Crossing rivers was another test of skill, for if the water was high, or "swimming," it was difficult as well as dangerous. If a river was low, there was danger of cattle being caught in quicksand. Ordinarily, if the lead steers were strung out and allowed to approach the water slowly, they would plunge in and head for the opposite bank. The herd willingly followed the leaders. Trail

N Bar herd crossing the Powder River in Montana, 1886. The N Bar was owned by E. S. (Zeke) Newman of El Paso, Texas. Photo by L. A. Huffman. Courtesy of the Amon Carter Museum of Western Art, Fort Worth

bosses learned not to push cattle into a river when the sun was low and facing them, for they would start milling halfway across, and many might drown.

The Red River was especially treacherous, for storms upstream often made it rise suddenly, even while a herd was crossing. More trail hands were drowned in the Red than any other river. The Cimarron was also difficult to cross, for it had a bottom of quicksand in which cattle bogged down if they stopped to drink. Pulling cattle out of quicksand was hard, time-consuming work. Some streams contained poisonous gypsum deposits that killed many cattle.

Often when a river was flooded over its banks a number of herds had to wait for it to subside. This happened at the Red

River Station crossing in the spring of 1871, when heavy rains raised the river over its banks until it was a mile wide. Mark Withers, who had earlier taken part in Joseph McCoy's wild west show, started from Caldwell County with twenty-two hundred head of mixed cattle. It rained every day, and the Colorado and Brazos rivers, which were usually easy for cattle to wade across, were both swimming when his herd reached them. When he was still three days' travel from Red River Station, Withers heard thousands of cattle bellowing. The sound grew louder the next day, and it never ceased.

Withers left his herd and rode ahead, to find the Red River a foaming torrent full of uprooted brush and trees. He saw a number of trail bosses and cowmen gathered there, including Shanghai Pierce. Pierce, whose voice could be heard farther than that of any other Texan, was doing the talking. There were sixty thousand cattle waiting to cross; Pierce urged everyone present to move his herd back ten or twelve miles. With so many outfits so close together, he said, if any herd started to run there

Abel H. ("Shanghai") Pierce, Texas rancher and trail driver. Western History Collections, University of Oklahoma Library

would be hell to pay, and all would lose money. It was clear that it would be days before any herd could cross, but none of the bosses was willing to drop back and risk losing his turn at crossing.

The first outfit that had reached the river was an all-Mexican crew with a small herd from Refugio County. After a few days the rain stopped and the sky cleared. Late in the afternoon the vaqueros drove a small bunch of steers down the cut and into the water, with one rider accompanying them. The powerful current swept them downstream; a submerged log shot to the surface, striking the vaquero's horse and unseating the rider. He tried desperately to grab a steer's tail but failed to reach it. Another vaquero spurred his horse into the current in a vain effort to save him; both men and the cattle were swept under.

A few nights later one of the waiting herds stampeded, and soon all of the cattle for miles around were milling. As Shanghai Pierce had predicted, everyone lost money, for cattle were crippled and killed, and it took ten days to separate the herds.

Dick Withers, like his brother Mark, was an experienced trail boss. In 1879, with ten cowboys, a cook, and a wrangler, he drove fifty-five hundred mixed cattle to Ogallala for J. F. Ellison. At the Red River one man was too sick to continue, and two quit. Although it was an unusually large herd, Withers eased it along with only a skeleton crew. At Dodge City he hired more cowboys and continued.

At Ogallala, Nebraska, Ellison instructed Withers to cut out one thousand cows, one thousand yearlings, and seven hundred two-year-old steers. When Ellison rode out to the herd, he found the cowboys cutting out some "long yearlings" as two-year-olds. "Dick," he warned Withers, "a Texan is going to receive those cattle and he knows ones from twos." But when Withers and the Texan classed the cattle, they agreed on eight hundred yearlings and nine hundred two-year-olds, which meant unexpected profits for Ellison. He was so pleased he bought supper for the whole crew and gave Withers train fare back to Texas.[5] Contracts calling for cattle of a certain age were filled by substituting younger ones when older cattle were scarce. It was surprising, cowboys wryly noted, how much cattle aged on the trail.

A trail boss always had to be prepared for the unexpected. In April 1879 a herd of Tom Snyder's steers started up the trail a short distance south of Victoria, with Dick Arnett as boss. As usual, early in the drive the cattle were nervous and easily stampeded, and on the second day the herd passed through the main street of Victoria. A woman saw them coming and was afraid that the steers would break down her fence and destroy her roses. She ran out to the fence, waving bonnet or apron at the cattle. It was said that cowboys feared nothing more than a good woman, and clearly the steers shared this feeling, for the leaders turned back and the rush was on. Only the quick thinking of trail boss Arnett saved Victoria from a Longhorn tornado. "Give way at all street crossings and let the cattle have room," he shouted. Dashing about and giving orders, he prevented the steers from taking short cuts through the houses. Several blocks of homes were surrounded by wild-eyed Longhorns, but they soon became quiet and were easily driven on through the town.[6]

The next night the cattle were bedded in a wide lane east of Gonzalez. The lane had high rail fences on either side, so night guards were stationed only at each end. During the night the herd stampeded and could not be checked. When the cattle were rounded up and counted the next day one hundred steers were missing. Four seedy-looking characters rode up and offered to bring in strays for one dollar a head, but accepted fifty cents instead. They brought in sixty, and it seemed likely that they had stampeded the cattle. The trail crew brought in twenty more, so they were only twenty short.

When the herd reached Fort Worth, Arnett held it over for a day while he and the cook bought everything needed for the five-hundred-mile trek to Dodge City. Several representatives of Fort Worth business houses rode up with whiskey, cigars, and similar gifts for the trail boss. All trail hands loved practical jokes, and on this occasion Arnett stayed with the herd while the cowboys indicated that gray-haired "Shug" Pointer was trail boss. Pointer had solemnly accepted the proffered gifts when one of the cowboys rode up and said, "Shug, the boss says come on, you lazy cuss, and get to work, or he'll turn you off at Fort Worth." All of the hands had a good laugh over the expressions of shock when the Fort Worth solicitors realized they had been taken in.

Tom Snyder rode the train to Dodge City ahead of the herd. Learning that many cattle in other herds had died from drinking gypsum water at several crossings, he sent a man to guide Arnett and the herd through the danger areas. At one of the bad crossings the cattle were thirsty, but the sight of dead cattle all around was proof that the water was poisonous. The men bunched the cattle near the crossing, then rushed at them shouting and waving slickers, to stampede them across the shallow stream. Even though some of the cattle tried to turn back to drink, the cowboys got the herd safely out of danger.

When they crossed the Cimarron near the Kansas line, Arnett learned that there was no more water for the cattle until they reached the Arkansas River at Dodge City, nearly one hundred miles away. The herd had been grazing along, making about twelve miles a day. Now it had to be pushed so as to cover the one hundred miles in four days. By the fourth day the cattle were staggering from thirst, and the herd stretched out five miles or more. Fortunately, it rained and small pools of water formed, which helped save them.

North of Dodge City there were daily rumors of Indian war parties in the area. Finally Arnett met some Texas cowboys with a herd of eight hundred horses they were taking to Ogallala, Nebraska, to sell to ranchers. The boss of the horse herd asked Arnett if he had seen any Indians. Arnett replied that he had not seen any, but had heard something about them every day. The boss of the horse herd admitted that he and his men had had so much trouble with sod-busters that they began spreading reports about Cheyenne war parties and then making night drives, knowing that men who feared an Indian attack would not interfere with the horse herd.[7]

Relations between trail bosses and Kansas sod-busters ranged from hostile to cordial, for although there was mutual resentment, each also had something the other needed. The settlers plowed furrows around their fields in place of fences, but Longhorns were not kept out of cornfields by scratches in the earth. When cattle crossed the furrows, the trail boss was fined for trespass.

But when night approached it was a different situation, for farmers offered fresh eggs, vegetables, and other inducements to trail bosses to bed their cattle on the farmers' land in order to obtain a supply of fuel for the coming winter. When the herds left the next morning the farmers guarded their donations "like a Texas man does a watermelon patch" until the cow chips were dry enough to gather and store.[8]

Before their trailing business became so large that they had to hire a number of crews, the Snyder brothers were their own trail bosses. They began by buying cattle on credit and trailing them to Abilene. Over the years Snyder herds were driven to New Mexico, Colorado, Nebraska, Wyoming, and Montana, where they helped stock new ranches.

The Snyders were pious folk, and they enforced strict rules of conduct for their cowboys. "First, you can't drink whiskey and work for us. Second, you can't play cards and gamble and work for us. Third, you can't curse or swear in our camps or in our presence and work for us." Once when Tom Snyder and his crew were riding south to pick up a herd at Victoria, a young man joined them. Soon he was cursing everything in sight, and for one so young his vocabulary was rich and varied and reasonably colorful.

Finally Tom Snyder stopped him. "Young man," he said, "we will be pleased to have your company if you will not swear so much, but if you cannot quit cursing, please fall behind or ride ahead of us. We propose to be gentlemen."

"Mister, is you a Christian?" the startled youth asked.

"I hope so."

"And a cow driver?"

"Yes. Why not?"

"That's awful damn strange," the boy shouted as he galloped away.[9]

Like the Snyder brothers, "Uncle Henry" Clare of Bee County was another trail boss who could not stand profanity. Whenever things went wrong his strongest expression was "O my stars, boys, don't let 'em run!"[10]

One of the best-known trail bosses was Albert Pickens ("Ab") Blocker, who trailed cattle year after year in the employ of his brother John. He had gone up the trail as a youth but reluctantly abandoned it one season to help his mother on her farm. After all the hard work involved in raising a crop of cotton, it sold for only four cents a pound. Ab gave up farming in

John R. Blocker, head of Blocker Brothers, trailing contractors. Western History Collections, University of Oklahoma Library

disgust and returned to the only life that suited him, and to his preferred diet of beef, potatoes, and whiskey.

The Blockers had the reputation of being hard taskmasters. One cowboy said that when working for the Blockers he could always count on "two suppers ever' night . . . one after dark and the second befo' sunup next mornin'." John Blocker possessed, nevertheless, an element of chivalry. When a widow tried to sell him one hundred steers for ten dollars a head he refused, but threw the steers in with his herd. After the cattle were sold he brought the widow fifteen hundred dollars. She tried to pay him the customary one dollar per steer, but he shook his head. "The boys didn't know they were in the herd," he told her.

During the few years he was married, Ab's wife shocked him by giving birth to a daughter. When a neighbor's wife asked Ab how she was doing, he replied, "Oh, she's just as porely as she can be. She's had everything from hollerhorn to a baby."

"Hollerhorn" (hollowhorn) was his term for any bovine ailment.[11]

The kinds of harassment trail bosses might face on the way north were experienced by Doc Manahan of Fairfield, Texas, when he delivered a herd of wild two- and three-year-olds to Fort Reno and other posts in 1873. Since the herd had been purchased by the government, Manahan had an escort of twelve troopers. In Llano County eight mean-looking armed men rode into camp; the leader claimed that the herd was on his land, and demanded fifty cents a day for horses and twenty-five cents for cattle. Doc Manahan pulled him off his horse and thrashed him, which was all the payment he got.

When Manahan's herd reached the Red River, it was rising, and he had to wait five days for it to subside. In Indian Territory, U.S. marshals told him that two weeks earlier rustlers had killed most of the men with a herd of fifteen hundred cattle and had stolen the entire herd. Across the Washita armed men demanded the right to cut the herd for strays. Well aware that this was a common trick of rustlers, Manahan ran them off.

After the herd had crossed the Cimarron a thunderstorm started a stampede that lasted three hours. In the morning Manahan counted his crew and the herd and found two men and thirty head of cattle missing. An Indian rode up and informed them that he had seen dead cattle at the foot of a cliff. With the dead cattle, Manahan discovered the bodies of his missing men, one a sergeant of the escort.

At the Kansas line more armed men rode up, claiming the right to inspect the herd for ticks, and demanding payment of twenty-five cents a head for the service. When Manahan threatened to have them arrested, they withdrew. Fake inspectors were common, not only at the Kansas border, but even at the Red River crossing. In 1873 two "inspectors" ordered a trail boss to pay fifty dollars apiece for two strays in his herd. He had his cowboys tie the men and throw them in the wagon, setting them afoot somewhere in Indian Territory.[12]

On the trail, strays, either from the range the cattle were passing through or from earlier herds, often joined the drive. After inspectors were placed at the Texas border, these animals were cut out. But trail bosses never objected to having strays accompany their cattle, for they could provide beef for the crew or for Indians who demanded a "wohaw" or two, or they could be sold in place of cattle lost on the trail. ("Wohaw" was what Indians thought ox drivers called their cattle). As one man remarked about unbranded cattle that joined his herd and refused to be turned away, "But it is remarkable the way these cattle persisted in following the herd. Naturally our sympathy was with them."[13]

William Jackson was bossing his own herd and crew when a stray with Ike Pryor's road brand joined his cattle. Jackson planned to turn the stray over to Pryor at Dodge City, but near Fort Sill a band of Kiowas or Comanches stopped him. The leader handed Jackson a slip of paper. It said to treat this Indian well and give him a beef, and there would be no trouble. Pryor had signed the note.

Chuckling to himself, Jackson called one of his men and told him to cut out Pryor's steer and give it to the Indians. It might seem that when a herd of two thousand steers was stretched out half a mile or more, finding any particular animal would be hopeless. But since trail cattle took approximately the same places every day, it required only a few minutes to locate the steer and cut him out.

After water holes or streams along the trail were fenced, cowmen were forced to pay for each head watered; in some cases they were refused water. In the early 1880s Shanghai Pierce accompanied one of his herds north, and found water scarce. When the thirsty cattle finally reached a water hole, local ranchers armed with Winchesters denied him water, even after he grudgingly offered to pay. He drove his cattle up the trail that night and bedded them down without water.

With a few reliable men Pierce rode back and drove off a herd of steers that belonged to the men who had refused him water. He ordered his men to push them hard toward Kansas, "till their tongues dragged the ground."

Several times the next day the ranchers rode up and asked to cut Pierce's herd for their lost cattle. It was customary, when a herd crossed another man's range, to let him inspect it for his strays. On this occasion Pierce was more obliging than usual, allowing them to take all the time they wanted, in order to give his own men more time to get the lost steers beyond reach. This continued for several days; each time Pierce was polite and agreeable. But on the fourth day, knowing that his men were safely away, he armed the rest of his cowboys. When the ranchers came again to cut his herd he said, "No damn grease sack outfit can trail cut my herd four successive days. Get goin'." Although it was dry, he solemnly remarked later, considering the "natural increase" of his cattle on the road, it turned out to be a profitable drive.[14]

One man started up the trail with his own herd from his ranch near Decatur in the spring of 1868. They camped a few nights later near Victoria Peak, northwest of where Bowie is now located. That night Comanches drove off the entire remuda except the night horses, which were tied near the wagon. The two men on the first guard saw the Comanche raiding party; knowing that in those days when a man lost his hair it was not all he lost, they preserved theirs by dashing all the way back to Decatur, where they breathlessly announced that Indians had killed everyone with the herd. The owner rode thirty-five miles back to his ranch, bought horses, hired two men, and was back with the herd by the next day.

When a trail boss allowed himself to be pushed into doing something against his better judgment, the results were likely to be disastrous. One held up his herd at the Canadian River when it was at flood stage. Because his men poked fun at him for being so cautious, he ordered the herd moved into the river, leading the way himself.

The river was not to be crossed that day, and the boss and his horse were swept under. When the men finally recovered his body, they found a letter from his wife in his coat pocket. In it she begged him not to try to cross rivers when they were flooding.

In 1874, Sol West was given charge of a herd belonging to his brother. They agreed on the selling price, and would split profits between them. Sol was one of the youngest men who ever bossed a herd up the trail, and no man with him was over twenty. Eager to be the first to reach market, he set out from Lavaca County on February 27 and had a difficult time because of blizzards which scattered the cattle. Worse than that, every horse froze to death and he had to replace the entire remuda. On his return his brother went over the expenses carefully and figured the profits to be a dollar and a half. He handed Sol seventy-five cents, asking if he planned to buy another herd or start a bank.[15]

Controlling men was occasionally a problem for trail bosses, especially when they had to hire strangers after a drive had started. In 1888, S. D. Houston was driving twenty-five hundred steers north from the Pecos River region, when he was obliged to hire four men. After visiting Fort Sumner he returned to the herd and saw only one man with it. The new hands were at the wagon, all of them armed. Houston got his own gun and ordered them to drop theirs. They obeyed. Houston immediately moved camp, leaving the four men behind with nothing but their saddles.

Short-handed, Houston had to leave the Pecos and cross the Staked Plain, a ninety-mile drive without water. He had the wrangler turn the remuda in with the herd and help with the drive. They reached the Canadian without losing any cattle. At Clayton, New Mexico, he hired a youth named Willie Matthews, who stayed with the herd until it was near the Colorado-Wyoming border and then quit because of homesickness. A short time later a lady visited the herd—it was the same Willie Matthews. She was the daughter of an old-time trail driver from South Texas who was determined to see for herself what "going up the trail" was really like.[16]

Among the best-known trail bosses was Dick Head, "one of the best cattlemen that ever came from Texas." He was a large, good-looking man with a black beard and "eyes that seemed to penetrate you."[17] He had trailed cattle to California, and he bossed dozens of herds to Kansas and beyond.

When Millett and Mabry contracted to deliver fifty-two thousand cattle at Ogallala and elsewhere in 1875, they hired Dick Head to serve as general manager for the drive. Head successfully supervised the seventeen herds on the trail, bringing them to Ogallala in good condition and earning his employers substantial profits.

Till Driscoll, another experienced trail boss, was in the employ of Schreiner and Lytle. When he trailed herds in the early 1880s he refused to allow his cowboys to carry guns. There was no longer danger of Indian attack, but when hungry Kiowas and Comanches demanded a "wohaw" or two for allowing cattle to cross their lands, it would have been easy for a trigger-happy cowboy to start a disastrous clash.

Driscoll never let his men crowd the cattle off the bed ground, but allowed them to remain until they were ready to graze off of their own accord. As a result there were few sorefooted cattle, and his herds arrived in good condition.

At the height of the trailing era, when a number of contractors sent up from five to fifteen herds each season, experienced trail bosses were in great demand. The techniques of trailing large herds were well known by this time, but there were still unforeseen dangers. Many drives were unsuccessful, and some were disasters, but that was in the nature of the business. The vast majority of herds made the journey in relative safety and without major calamities, some traveling all the way from the Rio Grande to the Dakotas.

The trail boss belonged to the era of the great cattle drives, and when it ended there was no longer any need for the type of field officer he represented. Like the mustang and the Longhorn, the trail boss vanished soon after barbed-wire fences began cutting up the Chisholm Trail.

CHAPTER 5

The Cook and His Castle

"Only a fool argues with a skunk, a mule, or a cook."

NEXT in rank and pay to the trail boss was the cook, lord of the chuck wagon, headquarters and home for trail hands. Trail bosses were only occasionally tyrannical toward the crew; chuck wagon cooks competed for the distinction of being known as the "techiest" one on the trail in any year. A widespread reputation of unrivaled crankiness was a source of satisfaction. No cook would admit, of course, that he was proud of the food he served, or that he greatly valued the crew's appreciation of his efforts.

It is hardly surprising that chuck wagon cooks were easily irritated much of the time. They had to feed eleven or twelve hard-working men three times a day regardless of weather or anything else; it was difficult enough when the weather was pleasant. Sandstorms, hailstorms, and drenching rains that soaked the fuel and left the ground under water often challenged the cooks' ingenuity. What they accomplished under the most adverse conditions was astonishing. The trail boss worried about the welfare of the cattle and horses—neither animals were given to complaining—but the cook was responsible for keeping the men well fed and reasonably contented. Nothing made tired men forget their weariness faster than a hot, tasty meal ready to eat the moment they slid from their saddles. Because of his impact on the crew's morale, a capable cook was essential, a man to be humored by all hands.

The chuck wagon was the cook's castle, and no man disputed this with impunity. "The space for fifty feet around the cook is holy ground," Bruce Siberts wrote, "and the cook is the Almighty. If things go wrong, he will raise hell. Maybe he will anyway. He is the only one who can cuss not only the hands but the boss too."[1]

From the two-wheeled ox carts that carried provisions and

Oscar Anderson's cook, Judith River roundup, 1910. Remuda is grazing in the background. Courtesy of Keith Anderson, Helena, Montana

served as mess wagons, the chuck wagon gradually evolved. Charles Goodnight is usually credited with inventing the chuck wagon, or at least with perfecting it. In the spring of 1866 he bought an army wagon with wide wheels and rebuilt it with the toughest wood he could find, such as thoroughly seasoned bois d'arc. The key element in Goodnight's design was the chuck box fitted across the rear of the wagon as a cupboard. The cover of the chuck box was hinged and had a dropleg, so that it served as the cook's work table.[2]

Each chuck wagon carried a water barrel strapped to one side, and a *cuna*, or cradle—"cooney," the cowboys called it, or "possum belly," or "the bitch"—slung under the wagon bed. The cooney was simply a cowhide suspended by the four corners to hold firewood or buffalo chips as an emergency fuel supply. It was the duty of the wrangler or the nighthawk to keep the cook supplied with firewood, but since the cowboys were also concerned they watched for dead branches they could rope and drag into camp.

Space for carrying food was extremely limited. Only easily

handled nonperishables such as cornmeal, beans, bacon or sow-belly, molasses, and coffee were the cook's regular supplies, while canned tomatoes and dried fruits were occasional luxuries. It required culinary artistry and imagination to concoct combinations of these limited ingredients that were not exactly like those of the day before or the day after. Whenever a beef was butchered the cook used only the choice cuts, for without refrigeration meat soon spoiled. In the early years buffalo, antelope, and wild turkeys enabled cooks to vary their menus. There were always lots of rabbits near the trail, but no cowboy would eat "nester food" unless he was starving, for "anybody that would eat rabbit would talk to hisself, and anybody who talks to hisself tells lies."[3]

Awakened usually by the last guard to go out to the herd, or by the built-in alarm clock in every trail cook's head, the cook arose before anyone else except the trail boss. When breakfast was nearly ready, he sent the wrangler out to bring in the remuda and called for the hands to "come and get it." The men ate, threw their dirty dishes and utensils into the "wreck pan" lying under the chuck box lid, turned their night horses loose, and saddled fresh ones from the remuda. Two men harnessed the chuck wagon mules and left them standing by the wagon. As they rode out to the herd, the last night guard headed for the wagon and a hasty breakfast. While the shifts of riders were eating, the cook prepared lunch to be served at noon when they threw the herd off the trail to rest.

After the last man had eaten, the cook washed dishes, pots, and pans while the wrangler loaded the Dutch ovens and the trail hands' bedrolls. Any cowboy who failed to tie up his bedroll and put it by the wagon might discover at night that his blankets still lay on his tarpaulin where he had left them that morning. The herd was already strung out grazing when the wagon and remuda left the camp ground and passed the slowly moving cattle. In five to seven miles they reached the place the boss had chosen for the noon stop. The cook unhitched his team, donned his flour sack apron, and began preparing the next meal.

At noon, while the cattle rested, the men rode to the wagon, half of them at a time, to eat a hurried meal and saddle a fresh horse. As soon as all had eaten and returned to the herd, the cook washed the dishes and then drove on to the place where the herd would be bedded down for the night.

At the night camp the wrangler dug a trench for the fire from six to ten inches deep and about two feet long. He placed the oven rack over the hole, and the cook suspended the Dutch ovens from it. Enough sourdough biscuits were made to last a day, so that they did not have to be baked at every meal. Some foods such as beans, which required four or five hours of cooking, were placed over the coals several times after meals had been served. Undercooked beans rattled noisily on the tin plates, a sound no cook wanted to hear. Chuck wagon cooks had much to remember and much planning for coming days if meals were to be ready on time. Since the herd wouldn't reach the bedding ground for several hours after the noon stop, the cook also had time to nap or hunt or fish.

At dark the cook pointed the wagon tongue toward the North Star. Before riding ahead each morning, the trail boss took note of the direction. This was usually the only "compass" available, and on cloudy nights it was undependable.

Few cooks were young, which may have accounted for some of their crankiness. Often they were crippled cowboys who could no longer do cow work. In the early years many were ex-slaves; others were Mexicans. Since the number of good trail cooks was never equal to the demand, good and bad they were humored and pampered regardless of color. One of the cardinal rules of the trail was that "only a fool argues with a skunk, a mule, or a cook."[4]

Cooks were usually paid more than cowhands, but no one complained, for there was no doubt that a good cook deserved all he was paid. His was a long, lonesome work day, and his hours of sleep were few. He had to drive an ox or mule team over rough ground and keep the wagon repaired until the herd was sold and delivered.

The cook also served as nurse and physician, handling all ailments from aches and pains to broken bones. Common complaints such as carbuncles, however, the cowboys treated themselves by placing a chew of tobacco on them. Among his limited

Roundup cook and pie biter—the wrangler—on a Montana range. Pot rack and hooks are in foreground, Dutch ovens on the right. Water barrel is on left side of wagon. Photo by L. A. Huffman. Courtesy of the Amon Carter Museum of Western Art, Fort Worth

Mealtime on the 2D range, Montana. Man in center is wearing Angora chaps. Cook has removed flour sack apron for photographer. The Montana Historical Society

supply of condiments the cook stored a few simple multipurpose medicines such as turpentine, liniment, quinine, and calomel, as well as some reasonably clean rags that could serve as bandages. His remedies for various ailments were typical of the folk medicine of the frontier. When dealing with dysentery caused by drinking alkali water, he boiled bachelors' buttons if they were in bloom, or fed sauerkraut if available. He might also make fry cakes using a batter of flour and salty water, or concoct a brew from the inside bark of cottonwood trees.[5] On occasion he was also a barber.

The food supplies chuck wagons carried were often decided as much by herd owners as by available space. Some owners, especially contract drovers, were tight-fisted, supplying mainly coffee, cornmeal, beans, and sowbelly. Others were as generous as conditions permitted, but perishable foods were, of course, out of the question, except for a meal or two when laying over at Fort Worth or when grangers in Kansas had eggs and vegetables for sale. In 1879 a Snyder herd on its way to Wyoming passed by Dodge City, where the boss and cook laid in a supply of provisions. Among the items purchased was a rare keg of pickles. Once the keg was opened, the men ate nothing but pickles until they were all gone.[6]

A staple of the chuck wagon was Arbuckle coffee, which came roasted but unground from Arbuckle Brothers of Pittsburgh. Strong, black coffee was served at all meals, and the pot sat on the coals all night so night herders could gulp down a cup before riding out to the herd.

Dried frijoles, or beans—red, pinto, or navy—high in protein and easily carried, were an important element in chuck wagon cooking. They were also inexpensive and easily obtained in Texas, although the cook had to spend some time picking out pebbles and other inedibles before soaking them overnight and cooking them for half a day or more.

The cook also kept a keg of sourdough fermenting; sourdough biscuits baked in a Dutch oven were daily fare that men were always ready to eat. The dough was also used to make crusts for other dishes and desserts.

Besides the "eatin' irons" and cooking utensils like pot

hooks, Dutch ovens, and coffee mills, chuck wagons also carried the cowboys' "war bags" containing their extra clothing. In addition there were usually an ax, a shovel, chains, and guns and ammunition, especially during electric storms, when the riders hastily got rid of everything metallic. When danger from rustlers or Indians threatened, the cook handed out the guns as the riders dashed by the wagon. Once when Comanches approached a herd, the boss had every gun passed out to the riders, leaving the cook with nothing but his butcher knife for defense. "By Jacks," he protested, "when it begins to thunder and lightning you fill this wagon full of six-shooters, but when the Indians are around the guns are all gone and who is going to protect me?"[7]

Trail bosses chose their cooks carefully and held onto good ones year after year if possible. But since there were more jobs than dependable cooks, bosses and crews were sometimes deeply disappointed. During a storm Mark Withers and his crew were out with the herd all night and much of the next day without rest and with only a "Spanish supper"—tightening the belt a notch or two. When the cattle were finally under control, Withers and half of the men rode to the wagon for coffee and a hot meal. There was not even a fire going, for the cook was rolled up in his blankets asleep. Somehow the infuriated Withers and his men refrained from shooting the cook, but Withers fired him and sent him on his way on foot.

On a drive from the Mexican border to Montana in 1896, five different cooks served part of the way with the herd. The cattle were shipped by rail whenever grass was scarce, and there were far too many towns where whiskey was available. When one cook was too drunk to work, the trail boss sacked him and hired another.[8]

It happened occasionally that after the chuck wagon had been rafted across a river, the water rose suddenly and spilled over its banks before the cattle had been crossed. In the spring of 1874 this happened at the Salt Fork of the Canadian River near the Kansas line. There were two wagons and twenty-four riders under trail boss Asa Dawdy. The wagons crossed safely, when the river suddenly rose and flowed a mile over its banks. Separated from the wagons for seven days without even their

"Mexican John," well-known XIT ranch cook in Montana. Photo by L. A. Huffman. Courtesy of the Amon Carter Museum of Western Art, Fort Worth

bedding, the men had nothing to eat but meat without salt.[9]

Most cooks had nicknames, often two. One was the name the cook wished to be called; the other was the cowboys' graphic but secret name for him. Bilious Bill, who cooked for the LU outfit, was always taking "sody" to settle his stomach. Vinegar Joe was known for his mock lemon pies made with vinegar. Bilious Bill and Vinegar Joe were once camped near each other on a roundup and each tried to outdo the other in a display of talents. A war between them was barely averted when Bilious Bill's pet, a retired chuck wagon mule that followed him everywhere, discovered the pies that Vinegar Joe had put out to cool and ate them all.[10] Dirty Dave was a cook whose name reflected his mania for washing dishes. "He's so plumb soap-

and-water crazy, so damn clean," a cowboy said, "that he's dirty."[11]

One cranky cook called Gray Jack lost his pipe, which only increased his irritability. At last, when he emptied the coffee pot, he found the missing pipe. Naturally, the cowboys could only congratulate him on his good fortune, for if they antagonized him they might find that there were worse things than coffee flavored with tobacco ashes and nicotine. A rough form of trail justice caught up with Gray Jack, for which he could blame no one but himself. One morning after all of the men had eaten and ridden out to the herd he discovered blankets and a tarp that had not been rolled up and tied according to the rigid trail etiquette. With a wicked grin Gray Jack attached tarp and blankets to a wagon wheel, which reduced them to shreds. When he looked for his own bedroll that night, he discovered that it was his own he had tied to the wagon wheel.[12]

In 1877 a trail outfit hired an inexperienced young man as cook at Fort Worth. One afternoon the boss told him to cook some dried apples for supper. He heaped a pot with dried apples and added water. As the apples swelled they overflowed the pot. Some of the cowboys saw the cook's predicament, and watched him. He dug a hole, and as the apples fell from the pot, he buried them in it. He had a new nickname next day—Apple Jack.[13]

One cook served dried apples until the men stopped eating them. Then he used them to make fried pies. When he heard a cowboy say, "Tromp on my corns and tell me lies, but don't pass me no apple pies," the cook was miffed. There was no more stewed fruit of any kind the rest of the trip.[14]

The tastiest dish chuck wagon cooks prepared was "son-of-a-bitch stew." Moved by sensitiveness unknown to old-time trail hands, modern writers usually call this popular dish "son-of-a-gun stew" or, more daringly, "SOB stew."

Son-of-a-bitch stew could be made only when a yearling had been slaughtered. The ingredients were brains, tongue, liver, heart, sweetbreads, kidneys, lights (lungs), and marrow gut, all cut into small pieces. Cooked in a Dutch oven, it made a rich, savory meal, especially with the cook's secret flavoring added. As one cook described it, "you throw ever'thing in the pot but the hair, horns, and holler." The longer it cooked the better it tasted, and a cook was mightily offended if anyone could guess all of the ingredients.[15]

After the early years big outfits often included both a night-hawk and a wrangler in the crew. The nighthawk herded the remuda all night, so that it was not necessary to hobble the horses as before. Days he drove the extra "hoodlum," or bed wagon, and doubled as a cook's louse, helping with the dish washing and other chores. When the wagons reached the next stopping place at noon or night, the nighthawk crawled into or under the wagon to catch what sleep he could.

Although the nighthawk remained one step lower than the wrangler in the hierarchy of trail hands, both boys were subjected to constant teasing. Nevertheless, at every opportunity the cowboys taught them to rope and other skills, and after one drive as wrangler a youth might graduate to riding drag the next year, a short step up the ladder.

One of the most bizarre cases of recruiting cooks occurred, according to legend, in Cheyenne, Wyoming, in the fall of 1876. A herd of Longhorns from Texas was crossing Wyoming on its way to an Indian agency in the Dakotas, when the cook died. The trail boss sent two cowboys into Cheyenne with orders to find a replacement and get him out to the herd pronto, for the season was getting late.

A short time earlier Custer and the Seventh Cavalry had made history on the Little Big Horn, and three Japanese generals and their aides had come to study the American Indian fighting army in the field. General Phil Sheridan had them with him in Cheyenne; the next stop would be Deadwood, where they would confer with General George Crook when he came in from his Sioux campaign.

Two Japanese captains in civilian clothes were wandering around Cheyenne one afternoon looking for excitement. They saw two dusty Texas cowboys riding up the street. The cowboys stopped and seemed to be discussing the Orientals. What they said was probably to the effect that "yonder's a couple of Chinks, and I hear tell that all them Chinks is good cooks."

The nighthawk in his nest. After herding the remuda all night he drove the hoodlum wagon to the next stop, then caught what sleep he could. Photo by L. A. Huffman. Amon Carter Museum of Western Art, Fort Worth

The captains watched impassively as the cowboys untied their lariats and shook out loops. In a moment the loops sailed through the air and pinned the captains' arms to their sides. They protested vigorously in their native tongue as the cowboys hauled them up behind their saddles, wheeled their ponies, and galloped out of town. When they reached the herd they dumped the two officers unceremoniously on the ground and pointed to the chuck wagon.

Not knowing a word of English, the captains were unable to explain that they were neither cooks nor Chinese. As the herd moved toward the Black Hills, the captains struggled with the four-mule team the wrangler had hitched to the chuck wagon.

General Sheridan was irritated but apologetic when he learned from the generals that two of their aides had mysteriously vanished. He took his guests on to Deadwood with him, explaining that his men would find the missing aides and bring them to Deadwood.

The trail-broken Longhorns moved steadily toward the Black Hills without protest, but the crew was on the verge of mass desertion. Their "Chinese" cooks were a disaster—they couldn't cook beans or biscuits. Even worse, they couldn't even brew a decent pot of coffee.

As the herd approached Deadwood, the boss managed to hire a stove-up miner who could make sourdough biscuits and boil beans. The boss paid off the "Chinese" cooks along with some uncomplimentary remarks they fortunately couldn't understand. The two captains were so happy to escape alive they declined to press charges. The trail boss shook his head in bewilderment as he watched them hurry up the road. Good cooks were sure hard to find.[16]

CHAPTER 6

The Cowboys

"Ma, do cowboys eat grass?"
"No, dear, they're partly human."
Rawhide Rawlins (Charlie Russell)

Cowboys, along with mustangs and Longhorns, were key but passive elements of the long drives and the cattle kingdom. Others made the financial arrangements; the cowboys simply did the work. They were, in fact, faceless youths on horseback, for most were known only by their first names even to their companions. Unless they wrote or dictated memoirs, today even their names are forgotten. As daring, graceful riders, nevertheless, they won a lofty place among American folk heroes, displacing the Daniel Boones and Kit Carsons of forest and mountain.

An estimated thirty-five thousand to fifty-five thousand men rode up the trails with cattle and horses. Perhaps one-fifth were black cowboys or Mexican vaqueros, and about one-third made the trip more than once. Nearly all were in their teens or early twenties when they first went up the trail; only cooks and bosses were likely to be over thirty.

Cowmen, as Lewis Atherton has pointed out, were as owners and managers considerably more important than the cowboys they employed. Despite this and the fact that ranching was the only American business that "evoked a literature, mythology, and graphic symbolism of its own," popular attention has always been focused on the cowboy rather than the cowman.[1]

Much has been written about these cowboys and the adventuresome, exciting lives they led. Most writers have viewed them favorably, whether accurately or imaginatively. A few, however, have taken a less flattering view of the hired men on horseback. Bruce Siberts felt that most of those in South Dakota were below average as humans.[2] Joseph G. McCoy, whose main

LU Ranch cowboys Thomas Aston and Dogie Taylor, 1889. Photo by L. A. Huffman. The Montana Historical Society

contact with cowboys was when they hit town at the end of the drive, spoke of them without trying to conceal his contempt. John Clay and Theodore Roosevelt both praised and criticized the cowboys they knew in Wyoming and the Dakotas.

Clay's criticism concerned the men who worked for the Scottish syndicate he represented, mainly in the Sweetwater valley of Wyoming. As the cattle came up from Texas to stock the northern ranges, he wrote, many cowboys came with them. The majority were well trained and no worse morally than the ordinary run of young fellows. But the great movement of cattle gave criminals and the indifferently honest the chance to move into new surroundings where they were unknown. The crew of the 71, (71 quarter circle), he added, was as mean a lot as ever got together, for though able, they were undependable, inclined to gambling, and held human life as of little value. It was, nevertheless, a pleasure to watch them sweep around a herd with an easy grace and careless abandon, never missing a point. Riding and roping were second nature to them. But cowboys usually degenerated and disappeared, he noted; old cowboys were rarely seen.[3]

Clay was especially disgusted with the cowboys who struck for higher wages on the 1884 Sweetwater roundup. He pointed out, with evident satisfaction, that the ones who quit all dropped out of sight, while those who remained loyal all became successful ranchers.[4]

Midwestern newspapers as well as the people of the Kansas trail towns mercilessly caricatured the youthful and unschooled Texas cowboys. The attitude of the people who profited by cheating and swindling the cowboys is not surprising, for one may drink milk without admiring cows. But these people saw cowboys only after months on the trail, not at work. Others, who watched them in action, generally respected them for their hard work and loyalty, their universal generosity, and their unfailing good humor.

The editor of the *Topeka Commonwealth* wrote on August 15, 1871,

> The Texas cattle herder is a character, the like of which can be found nowhere else on earth. Of course he is unlearned

and illiterate, with but few wants and meager ambition. His diet is principally navy plug and whisky and the occupation dearest to his heart is gambling. His dress consists of a flannel shirt with a handkerchief encircling his neck, butternut pants and a pair of long boots, in which are always the legs of his pants. His head is covered by a sombrero, which is a Mexican hat with a high crown and a brim of enormous dimensions. He generally wears a revolver on each side of his person, which he will use with as little hesitation on a man as on a wild animal. Such a character is dangerous and desperate and each one has generally killed his man. . . . They drink, swear, and fight, and life with them is a round of boisterous gayety and indulgence in sensual pleasure.[5]

Another view of the cowboy was that of salesman John McCoy, who arrived in Fort Worth in 1876:

The life of the cowboy is one of considerable daily danger and excitement. It is hard and full of exposure, but it is wild and free, and the young man who has long been a cowboy has but little taste for any other occupation. He lives hard, works hard, has but few comforts and fewer necessities.

He has but little, if any, taste for reading. He enjoys a coarse, practical joke, or a smutty story; loves danger but abhors labor of the common kind; never tires of riding, never wants to walk. . . .

One thing is certain about the cowboy. He is undoubtedly the Good Samaritan in the parable which was designed to hold up for commendation the most noble attribute of human nature. A Pharisee the true cowboy never is.

But the cowboy is more than a Good Samaritan. We do not read in the Bible that, in relieving the sufferings of the man who had fallen among thieves, the Samaritan parted with anything in which he was actually in need. The cowboy is not only generous when generosity costs him nothing, but he is generous when generosity involves actual personal hardship.[6]

Cowboys fought with guns but disdained fighting with their fists. They were common men without education, but, said Teddy Blue Abbott, "They set themselves away up above other people who the chances are were no more common and uneducated than themselves." They were fiercely independent, a quality that easterners and Britons like John Clay failed to comprehend. In Texas a cowboy's string of horses was virtually his personal property, and not even the owner dared tamper with them. Montana rancher Granville Stuart, unaware of this rigid custom, once sold a horse out of a man's string without consulting him. The offended cowboy asked for his time. When others explained his error to Stuart he was able to persuade the man to stay.

"Cowboys are ultra sensitive, diffident, and superstitious about anything that they do not understand," cowman Frank Hastings noted. "They possess a quality that is not necessarily courage, but rather the absence of fear."[7]

Cowboys were proud and sensitive, Abbott admitted. "But that sensitiveness on their part and the belief that their outfit was the best on earth was all to the advantage of the owners, and that was why John Clay was such a fool when he made that speech . . . in 1914, attacking the old-time cowpunchers."

What Clay said that provoked the rebuke was that "the chief obstacle on the range at that time was the cowboys, who were mostly illiterate, uncivilized; who drank and thieved and misbranded cattle, and with a kind of rough loyalty, never told on one another in their crimes."

"John Clay was a hard-fisted, money-loving Scotchman," Abbott continued, "who had no understanding of the kind of men who worked on the range. . . . They were all like a bunch of brothers. And if they weren't, they were no use as an outfit and the boss would get rid of them."[8] It should be added, in at least partial justification of Clay, that many men for whom sheriffs were looking in Texas and elsewhere changed their names and headed for Wyoming and Montana. Also, Texans were unable to generate much loyalty for eastern or British syndicates like the ones Clay represented.

In *The Story of the Cowboy,* Emerson Hough described the

"Teddy Blue" Abbott and cowboy artist Charlie Russell. The Montana
Historical Society

cowboy as simply a part of the West; anyone who did not understand the one could not possibly understand the other. "Never," he wrote, "was any character more misunderstood than he." People remember the "wild momentary freaks of man" but not the lifetime of hard work and loyalty. The cowboy should be seen in connection with his surroundings to know him as he actually was, "the product of primitive, chaotic, elemental forces, rough, barbarous, and strong." Then, "because at heart each of us is a barbarian," he will appeal to "something hid deep down in our common nature. And this is the way we should look at the cowboy of the passing West . . . as a man suited to his times."[9]

Cowboys were products of the great age of open range and free grass, of freedom-loving Longhorns and wiry little mustangs, and of the cattle kingdom stretching from the Rio Grande to the Mussellshell. As Don H. Biggers remarked about the cowboys of that era, "No class of men ever worked harder, endured more exposure, encountered greater danger, had fewer of life's common comforts or less time to devote to the cheerful side of existence."[10] Richard Irving Dodge added, "I doubt if there be in the world a class of men who lead lives so solitary, so exposed to constant hardship and danger, as this. . . . For fidelity to duty, for promptness and vigor of actions, for resources in difficulty, unshaken courage in danger, the cow-boy has no superior among men."[11]

The trailing of hundreds of cattle over trackless prairies, coping with thousands of rampaging buffalo, bands of playful mustangs that charged among the cattle, and resentful plains warriors came immediately after the Civil War. "It was," says western historian Clifford Westermeier, "the trail drives that made him a type—gave him his personality and exalted his specialized form of work. The trail drives produced a man unlike any other that had as yet appeared in the West."[12]

Because the increase in numbers of range cattle had been unregulated during the Civil War, postwar cattle trailing expanded almost explosively after the Chisholm Trail opened the way to profitable sales. Texans suddenly found themselves with vast herds of cattle and a distant, expanding market. The cattle had to be moved, but there was no comparable supply of experienced cowboys to move them. Early trail crews, or "crowds," were, therefore, mixtures of skillful Mexican vaqueros and equally adept ex-slave cowboys, on the one hand, and green boys fresh from farm or city on the other. Many of these youths later praised the Mexicans and black cowboys for their willingness to teach them to rope and ride and other skills needed for survival and success.[13] In a fairly short time, because of the many hours they spent in the saddle day after day, the greenies were converted into cowboys if they could stand the hard life as well as being the butt of camp jokes. Experienced cowboys who could be spared from ranch work for the trail were never numerous enough to fill the trail crews, so trailing continued to be a training ground for cowboys.

Young men came from far and near—East, Midwest, South—to work on Texas ranches and to "go up the trail." A large number of them soon realized that ranch life was not as pictured in dime novels, and quietly disappeared, but dozens of others realized their dreams. Some, like Ad Spaugh, left one-room sod-buster's cabins and wandered into cow camps, where amiable Texans took an interest in them and gave them the opportunity to begin doing a man's work at the age of fifteen.[14]

In the late 1860s most of the Anglo Texas cowboys were former Confederate soldiers in fact or by association, and they remained unreconstructed rebels at heart. Much of the end-of-the-trail boisterousness of Texas cowboys had undertones of Yankeephobia. The people of the Kansas cowtowns who eagerly separated trail hands from their money were all "no'therners" or "Yankees" to Texans. This same attitude carried over to eastern and British cattlemen and syndicates who hired Texans for their ranches in Wyoming, Montana, or the Dakotas. Texas cowboys, accustomed to cowmen who worked alongside them and treated them as equals, resented the absentee owners who regarded the cowhands as servants and whose visits to the ranches were like circuses. Only rarely could Texas cowboys develop a genuine respect for and feeling of loyalty toward these men.

Cowboy W. S. James was born in Tarrant County, Texas, in 1856, "the ugliest little bundle of humanity that could have been found in seventeen states and fourteen territories," he confessed. His father moved his herd to one of the western counties, probably Palo Pinto, where James grew up in the saddle.

"In reality the cow-boys might properly be divided into three classes," James wrote. "First, No. 1, the genuine, because of his true manhood, not only in his relationship to those with whom he is daily associated in handling cattle, but with all the world. One who has as much respect for the rights of others, though he be miles away, as for his immediate neighbors. I mean by that, a man who is strictly honest, one whom it does not affect in his general health to eat a piece of an animal of his own mark and brand."[15]

The second was the true type of western hospitality, liberal to a fault, especially in his moral views, who had an elastic conscience ready to serve him. His education often assisted him in interpreting to his own advantage the brands of cattle from northerly ranges. Eating his own beef "shore makes him sick."

James described the third class of cowboys—the typical cowboy—as "a big-hearted, whole-souled bundle of humanity, kind-hearted, generous to a fault, possessed of all the frailties common to mankind, and not the biggest rascal on earth by a jug full."

After the Civil War, Texas became the refuge of renegades from North and South, who were a greater scourge than Indians had ever been. It was they who gave the state a reputation for lawlessness and violence. Before the war, stealing cattle and horses was virtually unknown; horsestealing was regarded as worse than murder. Cow stealing, or rustling, began during the last years of the war.

Despite the undercurrent of Yankeephobia, any man who proved himself and who could take a joke was accepted. A genial old gentleman from the East came to Texas and bought two thousand choice steers. When he and some cowboys drove them to his camp, he wore a silk hat. He lay down for a nap under an oak tree, placing the hat on the ground by his side. He was awakened by the tramp of horses' hoofs as the cowboys rode into camp, and he listened to their talk.

"What must we do?" one asked.

"What is it?"

Circle Ranch roundup camp, 1906. Cutting hair was once one of the cook's skills. Here cook Ralph Waite is having his hair cut. The Montana Historical Society

"It's a bear."

"It's a venomous kypoote. It's one of those things that flew up and down the creek and hollowed 'wala wahoo' in the night time."

"Boys," one cowboy said, "it's a shame to stand peaceably by and see a good man devoured by that varmint." He called, "Look out there, mister, that thing will bite you," and drew his pistol. The old gentleman "got a ten cent move on him" and didn't stop to get his hat. By the time he was ten or fifteen feet away, every man had put a bullet or two through the hat, shooting the crown off.

Finally one of the cowboys dismounted and, with a stick, cautiously turned the hat over. "Boys, it's shore dead," he said. The old gentleman had a hearty laugh, called the cowboys to his wagon, and took out a jug of "sixteen-shooting liquor." Together they celebrated the death of the terrible varmint. One of the cowboys lent him a hat until they could chip in and buy him one, the best to be had. After three days on his new ranch, everyone, including the cook, was ready to fight his battles for him. It would have been a far different story if he had been angry over what they had done. They would simply have told him that if he brought wild animals into camp he could expect that they would be killed.

Before the Civil War, slaves were valued far more than cowboys, as one incident in Abel "Shanghai" Pierce's early ranch life illustrated. One of the most powerful of Texas cowmen after the war, Pierce recalled that as a young man working for W. B. Grimes he and a slave cowboy named Jake drew straws to see which of them got to ride an outlaw dun horse. Jake won, but the outlaw fell on him, leaving him stretched out unconscious on the ground. Grimes's aunt had been watching, and she concluded that Jake was dead. "There's $1500 gone, Bradford!" she shouted at Grimes. "Why didn't you let Abel Pierce ride that horse instead of Jake?"[16]

Some youths who aspired to be cowboys came from as far away as the British Isles, and a few of the successful ones wrote or dictated memoirs, which help us visualize cowboy life as they saw it. Among them was Frank Collinson, who came to San Antonio from England in 1872. There he went to work on John T. Lytle's ranch south of the city. Two ex-slave cowboys, both top hands, taught him every step in the process of breaking broncos and handling cattle. Collinson became a top hand and spent the rest of his life on the plains.

In 1874, Collinson went up the trail with a herd of thirty-six hundred of Lytle's steers to the Red Cloud Sioux Agency, then at Fort Robinson, Nebraska. The herd was composed largely of big brush steers that had been purchased in small bunches from many ranchers. Collinson considered the trail drive as nothing but hard work, though others like Teddy Blue Abbot viewed it differently.

Abbott had accompanied his family from England to Nebraska in 1871, when he was eleven. His first trailing experience was in 1873, when he accompanied his father to Texas to buy three hundred big steers from John R. Blocker. His father doubled his money on the cattle, breaking some to sell as oxen by yoking them and tying their tails together while they tore up the pasture for several days.

Although there were many Texas cattle and cowboys in Nebraska at that time, there was nothing north of Ogallala except Indians and buffalo. Texas cowboys were, according to Abbott, a wild, reckless breed, and he seems to have fitted in with them very well. His father was a tyrant, but the Texans were the most independent class of men on earth. They taught Abbott to ride and rope.

Abbott left home for good when he was eighteen, while his father and brothers continued the struggle to raise crops. Only one brother chose another career, said Abbott, "and he ended up the worst of the lot—a sheepman and a Republican."[17]

Because he arrived in Montana with a trail herd from Texas, Abbott was always regarded as a Texan. There was nothing about him to make him appear to be anything else, for like most Texas cowboys he was ready for any prank or other activity that tempted him. On one occasion he rode to New Mexico to help Bill Charlton receive a herd of seven hundred "wet" horses at the Rio Grande. Charlton paid the Mexican vaqueros three dollars a head for the stolen horses, then drove them to Nebraska and sold them to settlers for twenty-five to thirty dollars apiece.

Abbott's worst experience was helping the FUF crew gather wild brush cattle. Totally unprepared or equipped for brush popping, Abbott saw his clothes torn to shreds, and he picked thorns out of his knees all the way to Kansas. He swore never to go near brush country again.[18]

Unlike his countryman, Collinson, Abbott thoroughly enjoyed life on the trail. Some of the accounts of hardships were accurate, he admitted, "but they never put in any of the fun, and fun was at least half of it." In his later years he grumped that the famous collection *Trail Drivers of Texas* sounded like a bunch of preachers.

Montana cowboys at Big Sandy, around 1890, all looking like "strong, silent men." The Montana Historical Society

Another young man who headed west to become a cowboy was James Henry Cook, who in the early 1870s got his first job at Ellsworth, Kansas, working for a cowman holding a herd there. When the outfit returned to San Antonio, Cook went along. There he hired on with Ben Slaughter's foreman, John Longworth, to gather brush cattle. All of the other members of the crew were Mexican vaqueros; without them no cow hunt in the brush could succeed.

Even before they got into action Cook began learning some of the things a cowboy needed to know, such as providing beef when in camp. As they were preparing to head into the Brasada, Slaughter told Cook to kill a stray for beef. Cook leveled his rifle at a fat heifer.

"Hold on, young man, hold on," Slaughter said with some irritation. "Don't you see that's a T-Diamond?"

"Yes. Whose brand is that?"

"I reckon it's my brand. We don't kill that kind in this country. Kill an LO or a WFC (any brand but his own); they taste better."[19]

The vaqueros, who were paid only ten dollars a month while Cook received twelve dollars, generously taught him everything he needed to know, from making rawhide hobbles and braiding rawhide reatas to handling broncos and catching mossy horn outlaws in the brush. Under their tutelage Cook became a cowboy.

Like many young men, Cook was eager to go up the trail. When he learned that trail boss Joel Roberts was hiring, he asked for a job. Roberts knew of Cook's reputation as a marksman and hired him.

On his first trip up the trail Cook served as wrangler during the day. He also took his turn at night herding, and soon learned a lesson in the dangers of curiosity. Circling the herd he noticed an old black cow that continually grazed away from the others. Finally, after she had been turned back a number of times, she lay down, still away from the herd.

As he rode on his rounds Cook passed nearer and nearer to the black cow, wondering how close she would let him come. Finally he reached out and touched her neck with his boot. With a loud snort she bounded into the herd; the cattle were already on their feet and running, for the moment she snorted there was a roar and clash of horns and hocks and a trembling of the earth. Sleeping men knew instinctively what to do, for the roar of a stampede was like no other sound. Every man pulled on his boots and ran for his night horse; in moments the whole crew was racing through the night toward the sound of running cattle.

In the morning the cattle were strung out and counted; about five hundred were missing, causing a delay of several days while the strays were rounded up and more cattle were added from other Slaughter herds to replace the missing ones. Like many trail hands who caused stampedes through some act of foolishness or carelessness, Cook never admitted until years later that he had started the cattle running.[20]

Baylis John Fletcher was born in Williamson County at the edge of the Texas hill country; in 1879, at the age of nineteen, he rode up the trail with a herd belonging to his neighbor, Captain Tom Snyder.

In Indian Territory the trail boss, Dick Arnett, roped a wild mustang, which hit the end of the rope so hard it threw Arnett's horse. It fell hard on Arnett's right leg, reinjuring a wound he had received during the Civil War. Badly crippled, Arnett had to lie in the wagon for a week. It was then, when he was working with a crew of untrained trail hands, each acting as his own boss, that Fletcher became fully aware of the need for a competent trail boss in absolute control of herd and men. Fortunately, a man Tom Snyder sent to guide them through the saline and gypsum region took charge of the herd until Arnett recovered.

Another Texan who spent his life in the saddle was G. R. (Bob) Fudge, who was born in Lampasas County in 1862. When he was ten, his father, mother, sister, two brothers, and two aunts and uncles headed for California with one thousand steers and two hundred horses. In New Mexico, Comanches killed one uncle and ran off the cattle and all but four horses. Soon after that all but Fudge, his mother, and two brothers died of smallpox. The survivors returned to Texas.

At the age of twelve Fudge went to work for a rancher, and

was on his way to becoming a rarity in those days, a 250-pound cowboy. In 1881, at the age of nineteen, he helped trail a Higgins and Shankin herd to Colorado, and the following spring rode with a Blocker herd to the Little Big Horn country of Montana. Fudge made many trips up the trail, and worked eighteen years for the XIT ranch on its Montana range. The wildest trip he ever made was driving eight hundred horses to Wyoming, for they stampeded every night, making as much noise as a freight train.[21]

For several years during the height of the cattle kingdom, becoming a cowboy was almost a passion among eastern college men. Despite their genteel background some of them readily adapted to the hard life and became as skillful riders and ropers as their Texan instructors. A few young easterners like Edgar Beecher Bronson even won the respect of the Texas cowboys.

Unlike many aspiring cowboys who headed for Texas to learn the trade, Bronson went to Wyoming in June 1872. His friend Clarence King gave him a letter of introduction to his partner, N. R. Davis. Bronson arrived in Cheyenne with his cowboy outfit already purchased, his first mistake. Davis looked him over, barely concealing his contempt at the sight of laced boots, leggings, short hunting spurs, little round felt hat, and Colt .45. He steadied himself, drew his breath, and ordered Bronson to get rid of everything but the pistol. Starting Bronson almost in his underwear, Davis got him properly outfitted with a bridle, forty-pound saddle, rawhide lariat, California spurs with two-inch rowels, high-heeled boots, heavy leather chaps, and a big hat. For the roundup Davis also had him buy a tarpaulin, a buffalo robe, and two blankets. Then they set out for the ranch in a buckboard pulled by two half-broken broncos that spent more time in the air than on the ground.

On the way Davis gave Bronson a pithy but positive lecture on what he could expect. "I'm not going to favor you," he said. "You've got to take your medicine with Con Humphrey's outfit, and he's about as tough a rawhide as ever led a circle. But he always gets there, and that's the only reason I keep him. It's lay close to old Con's flank, Kid, and keep your end up or turn in your string of horses. On the round-up no soldiering goes; sick or well, it's hit yourself in the flank with your hat and keep up with the bunch or be set afoot to pack your saddle; there's no room in the chuck wagon for a quitter's blankets, and no time to close herd sick ones. So for heaven's sake don't start out unless you have the guts to stand it."[22]

Bronson assured him that while he might be unhandy at the new work, the moment he found he was in the way he'd turn in his horses and leave.

"I'm tally branding this summer," Davis continued in a more kindly tone, "making a tally or inventory of all our cattle and horses for an accounting and settlement with my partner. The corrals are full of cattle and it will take all day tomorrow to run through the chutes and hair-brand. The next morning Con starts his outfit down Willow to round up the Pawnee Butte country. I'll pass you up to Con tonight, and what he makes of the new hand will depend on what he finds in it. We'll dump your blankets and tricks at the chuck wagon, and you can make down among the boys. Earlier you start the sooner you learn— and that, I guess, is what you're here for. Don't mind the boys. They'll rough you a lot, but most of it will be good-humored. If any get ugly, you'll have to call them down, that's all."[23]

There was a fire blazing at the end of the chuck wagon, with about sixteen cowboys sitting around it, eating beef, beans, and biscuits from tin plates, and drinking strong coffee from tin cups. They were all ages, from sixteen to sixty, but most were under thirty. While no life of greater privation and hardship existed than that of cowboys, no merrier lot ever lived, for they joked constantly about every condition of life from cradle to grave. Bronson helped himself to a plate of food, but he couldn't bring himself to eat much.

"Kid," drawled Tobacco Jake, "ef you reckons to tote that full grown gun all day tomorrow, yu better ile yer jints with sow belly an' fill up all th' holler places inside yu with beans an' biscuits; yu shore look like yu hadn't had no man's grub in a month."

Bronson admitted that he had been something of an invalid, but he had recuperated, even if his physical condition was not yet up to par.

"Look yere, Kid," Jake said, "ef yu cain't talk our langwidge, you jus make signs. What'n hell yu trying' to say, anyway?"

This sort of chaff went on and on, until Bronson began to feel hot under the collar, when he heard the friendly voice of Tex Fuller. "Fellers," Tex said quietly, "jest shet y'r yawp, pronto! Let the kid alone—it's me sayin' it. Course he ain't goin' to keep up with no leaders on th' circle, but I've got a fool idea he won't be so far behind we'll lose him none." Tex spoke softly, but everyone listened, and there were no more comments that night, only a few whispers and snickers.

The next day the great corrals were filled with range cattle, old and young and of all the colors characteristic of the old Longhorn stock of South Texas. There were also traces of other breeds, the dark red and greater bulk of the Durham cross, Herefords, and even a few Angus. All were wild, with blazing eyes and rattling horns, surging threateningly back and forth between the corral fences.

Along one side of the corral was a narrow branding chute long enough to hold twenty animals. At one end of the chute was a small pen; the other end opened onto the prairie. Men on foot drove cattle from the main corral into the small pen and then pushed them into the chute. Two or three men with hot irons quickly branded them, then turned them loose. Except for an hour off for the midday meal, this work continued all day.

The work was hard and perilous, but all the men except the ill-natured foreman remained playful and joking. Bronson received both mock sympathy for his weakness and real anxiety for his safety. If an angry beast charged his way, others pushed him aside and took his place. They even mopped his sweating face with bandannas. That night Bronson thoroughly enjoyed the beans and biscuits and easily slept on the lumpy mattress of buffalo grass. The next day the wagon crew moved out on roundup; Bronson soon learned that Davis had assigned him five unusually good horses to be entrusted to a tenderfoot.

Roundup boss Con Humphrey knew cattle and horses, but hated all humans, including himself. The cowhands could see merit in Humphrey's self-hate, for to know him was not to love him. The danger was in Humphrey's taking his hatred out on

someone like Bronson, who might not be able to defend himself.
Bronson started out on circle with the others, which meant riding at top speed for half a day, pushing all of the cattle toward the center. It was a brutal way for a tenderfoot to harden his saddle muscles, for, as Bronson admitted, the old cow saddle gave him "harder cramps and tenderer spots in more parts of the anatomy than any punishment conceivable short of an inquisition rack."[24] By night every movement was agony, but his appetite and capacity for sleep astonished him. Within a week he was hardened to the work and confident of his ability to ride.

As Bronson's confidence grew he was determined to demonstrate what he had learned about handling bad horses, to convince the men that he no longer needed to be looked after. A big yellow-eyed, Roman-nosed, heavy muscled buckskin called Walking Bars was the worst outlaw in the whole ND outfit. The horse's name came from the motion of the walking bars, or beams, of side-wheel river boats. Bronson, through an uncontrollable surge of courage or foolhardiness, decided to start with the worst horse available.

Walking Bars was in the string of a slender, wiry little vaquero named José, whose skill enabled him to handle the big horse with disarming ease. Using an outlaw for cow work simply compounded one's problems, however, and José had grown tired of the constant battle. He was shocked beyond belief, therefore, when Bronson offered to swap the best horse in his string for the ornery buckskin.

"Madre de Dios! muchacho, he keela you, keela you sure," he exclaimed, but when he saw that Bronson was serious, he added, "but if you weesh, you heem have, *y que Dios te aguarda!* (and may God protect you!)."

At noon, when it was time to saddle fresh mounts, Bronson roped Walking Bars while the cowboys looked on in silence. After a hard battle Bronson worked his way up the rope and stuck a lump of sugar in the surprised horse's mouth, then easily bridled him. Unbelieving, the cowboys watched while the outlaw stood quietly.

Getting the saddle on required considerable diplomacy and caution, for Walking Bars was well known for his skill in whirling and kicking. When the saddle was on, one of the awed cowboys remarked, "Ya shorely has a medicine bag fo' outlaws hid about you."

When Bronson swung into the saddle and the horse walked off quietly, the cowboys shouted their approval, thereby breaking the spell. Walking Bars suddenly remembered that he had a reputation to uphold; he tucked his head between his front legs and hit the air, coming down with earth-jarring force. Bronson managed to hang on until the horse stopped, as if it suddenly remembered the sugar lump, then quietly trotted off after the other cow horses. Tex turned to another cowboy. "Lew," he asked, "does yu allow it's loco or sense an' sand th' Kid's sufferin' most from?"

Con Humphrey, probably because Bronson was the only one of the crew he didn't fear, roped Walking Bars and removed the hackamore that had been left on him permanently as a halter. It was impossible, Humphrey knew, to bridle the horse without the hackamore in place. Bronson would get himself killed or at least look ridiculous in the attempt to bridle Walking Bars.

José was the first to know what Humphrey had done. He found Bronson and told him to kill Humphrey, eagerly offering to help. They would have to "go on the scout" afterward, he said, meaning hide from the law. Bronson was trying to figure a way out of the difficulty without either killing Humphrey or letting him get away with it, when his friend Tex rode up. Tell Con if he ever fools with your horse again you'll have his hide and scales, Tex advised him. Ride in and stay real close to him, so if he reaches for his gun you can crack him good over the head. One of the Texas ranch codes was that no man, foreman or owner, could tamper with a cowboy's string, and Humphrey had openly violated that code. Some Texans would have killed him for it.

He would stay near, Tex said, but he would let Bronson make his play, " 'n ef he gets yu, Kid, it'll be th' last gun game he'll git to ante in, 'n' then it'll be Tex fer the scout. But we'll make her a squar' play; I won't chip in 'fore yu're down."

With this assurance, Bronson rode close to Humphrey and warned him to leave his string alone or he'd have trouble. Humphrey's rage was almost beyond control when he heard a horse whinny. He looked around and saw Tex sitting on his horse about seventy-five yards away, his Winchester .44 partly raised. Tex might have been looking at the cattle, for his face was expressionless.

This sight was a great inspiration to Humphrey to bring his temper under control. He had only been funnin', he lied, and meant no harm. He would have the boys rope Walking Bars and replace the hackamore, he said, and rode away. "Allus knew he was a coyote," Tex told Bronson on his way back to the drag.

Humphrey was not through trying to bring Bronson down; he ordered him to drive a cow and calf to the ranch headquarters, at least twenty miles away, across the unfamiliar Iliff range. There was no trail and few landmarks, and the range was covered with cattle. It would have been difficult for two men, but Bronson had no choice.

Again Tex came to the rescue. Ease her along gently the whole way, he advised, so she will naturally think she has business there she's bound to tend to herself. By keeping calm and riding hard only when necessary to keep the cow from joining others, Bronson eased her along, trying to follow the landmarks Tex had described.

A heavy rain struck as they neared the ranch headquarters; the weary cow and calf became unmanageable. Bronson rode on to the ranch for a fresh horse. Davis saw him coming and wanted to know why he was there. When Bronson explained, Davis was furious. "Well, where is she, anyhow?" Bronson told him he'd left the cow and calf about two miles away when the storm struck. "Well, I guess you'd better get her," Davis told him.

Saddling a fresh horse, Bronson had closed a corral gate on the cow and calf by the time the sun set. Davis walked up as Bronson unsaddled. "Kid," he said, "you've sure won puncher spurs today." This feat and his mastering of Walking Bars gave Bronson a reputation in Wyoming that enabled him, an eastern tenderfoot, to hire a crew of Texas cowboys when he established a ranch of his own.[25]

Although there were wide differences of opinion concerning cowboys and their traits of character, on the range they were generally an admirable group. Their wages were invariably low; they were attracted not by the pay but the way of life. As a rule they were reserved around strangers, and they distrusted any man who talked a lot at the first meeting. Meanness, cowardice, dishonesty, and chronic complaining were not tolerated on the range or the trail.

Teddy Roosevelt, a Dakota rancher in the 1880s, observed that cowboys were smaller and less muscular than men who wielded ax or pick, but they were as hardy and self-reliant as any. Peril and hardship were part of their daily life. The struggle for survival on the range, Roosevelt noted, was sharp; the West was no place for softies.

"Some cowboys are Mexicans," Roosevelt added, "who generally do the actual work well enough." Roosevelt was expressing an unacknowledged bias of his own, for Mexican vaqueros were unsurpassed in roping and riding and handling cattle. Some Texans, Roosevelt continued, "among whom the intolerant caste spirit is very strong," did not employ many Mexicans. Others relied heavily on them. Mexicans were, Roosevelt admitted, the best ropers, but some Texans were not far behind them. A top hand could, without assistance, rope, throw, and tie a cow or steer in a remarkably short time.[26]

A contemporary of Roosevelt commented in the *Providence Journal* that cowboys were a strange mixture of good nature and recklessness. "You are as safe with them on the plains as with any men," he wrote, "so long as you do not impose upon them. They will even deny themselves for your comfort, and imperil their lives for your safety. But impose upon them, or arouse their ire, and your life is of no more value in their esteem than a coyote. Morally, as a class, they are . . . blasphemous, drunken, lecherous, utterly corrupt."[27]

Before he married one of Granville Stuart's daughters and moved up from cowboy to cowman, Teddy Blue Abbott was a typical cowboy, and he explained the range riders' attitudes toward women. In Miles City, he said, the cowboys would go to town and "marry" a girl for a week, to be with her day and night. They couldn't do that elsewhere, he noted, without risking arrest. "I suppose those things would shock a lot of respectable people. But we wasn't respectable and we didn't pretend to be, which was the only way we was different from some others." Cowboys had their own strict code. "I never knew of but one case where a fellow cheated one of those girls," Abbott continued,

and I'll bet he never tried it again. He came up the trail for one of the N Bar outfits . . . and he went with Cowboy Annie for a week. Then he got on his horse and rode away, owing her seventy dollars. First he went back to the Niobara, but the foreman of the outfit heard of it and fired him, then he went down in Texas, but they heard of it down there and fired him again. And the N Bar fellows took up a collection and paid what he owed, because they wouldn't have a thing like that standing against the name of the outfit.

That shows you how we were about those things. As Mag Burns used to say, the cowpunchers treated them sporting women better than some men treat their wives.

Well, they were women. We didn't know any others. And any man that would abuse one of them was a son of a gun. I remember one P.I. [pimp] beat up on his girl for not coming through with enough money . . . a fellow I know jumped him and half-killed him. The man hadn't done nothing to him. It was none of his business. It was just the idea of mistreating a woman.[28]

Edgar Rye, who also knew the old-time Texas cowboys, wrote, "All honor to the Texas cowboy, living or dead. With all his faults his virtues were many." Generosity, he said, was characteristic, despite the daily hardships, for "nowhere on the earth is true manhood put to a more severe test." Hospitality was another virtue, for there was always a "rough, cheerful sincerity about the cowboy's manner that made one feel at ease." In a cowboy camp, he added, "a stranger always received a hearty welcome."[29]

What were the open range, trail-driving cowboys really like? The consensus among those who actually knew them was that they were hard-working youths who reveled in life in the saddle, and who chose to follow it for a time despite the poor pay and hardships. Their virtues were loyalty, fearlessness, generosity, and constant good humor. Their vices were occasional drunken sprees and an unwillingness to live by the Puritan code of thrift. Their proudest boast was "We held the herd."

The so-called bad men of the cowtowns should not be confused with cowboys, although a few trail hands like Sam Bass did graduate to robbing trains and other shady activities. Most cowboys carried guns, for they felt half-naked without them, but they did not make a habit of using them on one another.

There may be a parallel between the romantic view of the cowboy and of the wild mustang. From a distance the wild horses, with arched necks and tossing manes, clearly gloried in their freedom and appeared to be the most superb animals on earth. Once caught and broken to the saddle, however, they were simply ordinary cow ponies. Like the wild horses, cowboys in action were quite different from cowboys out of their element.

Charles Goodnight, one of the major cowmen who had gotten his start as a trail boss, summed up his feelings about his trailing days and paid the cowboys perhaps their finest tribute. "Taken all in all," he said, "my life on the trail was the happiest part of it. I wish I could find words to describe the companionship and loyalty of the men toward each other. It is beyond imagination. The cowboy of the old days is the most misunderstood man on earth. Few people of the younger generation realize that the Western men—the cowboys—were as brave and chivalrous as it is possible to be. Bullies and tyrants were unknown among them. They kept their places around a herd under all circumstances and if they had to fight they were always ready."[30]

Cowboys sweeping gracefully around a herd made an inspiring sight, as John Clay admitted. Away from the range and on foot, the cowboy lost his aura. But there can be no doubt that the cowboy of the trail-driving era captivated Americans as no other folk hero before or since. When all else is said, this fact remains.

CHAPTER 7

Longhorns and Mustangs

"Wherever cattle were driven, it took the
Spanish horse to do the work."

Frank Collinson

WHEN Anglos migrated to to Texas in the early nineteenth century, there were thousands of Spanish cattle running wild all
across South Texas between the Nueces and the Rio Grande,
along the San Gabriel and San Saba rivers and other tributaries
of the upper Colorado. They could be found from the Louisiana
border to the upper Brazos, and they were equally at home on
the coastal plains and in the brush country.

The early descriptions of these wild cattle suggest some,
though not all, of the colors and other characteristics of the later
Texas Longhorns. Not all the cattle in the region were wild, for
some were kept under control on old Spanish ranches as well as
Anglo establishments. In 1832, Charles Sealsfield visited the
ranch of a Kentuckian named Neal, which was a few miles off
the Harrisburg-Austin road. While Sealsfield was visiting the
ranch, Neal and three Negro cowboys were rounding up twenty
or thirty steers to take to New Orleans. Sealsfield accompanied
them; they rode four or five miles and then, Sealsfield reported,
"We came in sight of a drove, splendid animals, standing very
high and of most symmetrical form. The horns of these cattle
are of unusual length and in the distance have more the appearance of stag's antlers than bull's horns. We approached the herd
first to within a quarter of a mile. They remained quiet. We rode
around them and in like manner got in the rear of a second and
third drove and then began to spread out so as to form a half
circle and drive the cattle toward the house." About this time
Sealsfield's mustang pitched him off. He was lost for several days
and as a result missed the rest of the roundup.[1]

During the rebellion against Mexico many cowmen were

forced to abandon their ranches, and their herds scattered. No doubt it was during this time that the development of the Longhorns began, for they were a mixture of Anglo and native, or Spanish, stock. It was a matter of survival of the strongest, without the guiding hands of cattle breeders and the matching of pedigrees. After independence had been won, ranchers organized cow hunts to rebuild their herds.

In 1840, James Huckins saw many cattle along the San Bernard. "I have never seen cattle superior to those I find in this region," he wrote. "They are large and in good condition presenting horns of a very great size."[2] The San Marcos region was also stocked with wild cattle, but they were so shy and alert that only the most expert hunters could get a shot at them. The settlers' cattle were quick to join the wild ones at any opportunity, and thereby continued contributing to the development of the Longhorn.[3] Although the colors of these wild cattle were not stated, it seems likely that those nearest the settlements were already mixed with stock the Anglos introduced.

Farther from the settlements, near the sources of the San Gabriel and the Brushy and along the Leona, San Saba, Llano, and Little rivers, the wild cattle were still unmixed Spanish stock. An anonymous visitor in the 1840s called them a "singular" breed. They differed in form, color, and habits from all the varieties of domestic cattle in Texas. "They are invariably of a dark-brown color with a slight tinge of dusky yellow on the tip of the nose and on the belly. Their horns are remarkably large and stand out straight from the head. Although these cattle are generally much larger than the domestic cattle, they are more fleet and nimble and when pursued often outstrip horses that easily outrun the buffalo. Unlike the buffalo, they seldom venture far out into the prairies, but are generally found in or near the forests that skirt the streams in that section. Their meat is of an excellent flavor and is preferred by the settlers to the meat of the domestic cattle. It is said that their fat is so hard and compact that it will not melt in the hottest days of summer."

Some men believed that these cattle were of a distinct breed indigenous to America. "But," according to this observer, "as these cattle are now found only in the vicinity of the old

Within the image (handwritten on photo): WEIGHT 1700 EXHIBITED AT PARIS EXP 19 ... (1) TEXAS STEER HORNS 9 FT 7 IN. FROM TIP TO TIP LARGEST IN THE W...

An old Texas Longhorn steer, with horns measuring nine feet seven inches from tip to tip. Steers' horns grew much longer than those of bulls or cows. Courtesy of the Oklahoma Historical Society

missions, it is much more probable that they are the descendants of the cattle introduced by the early Spanish adventurers." Attempts to domesticate them, the unknown writer added, were so far unsuccessful.[4]

Although the native cattle already had horns long enough to attract the attention of those seeing them for the first time, there is at least a slight possibility that this tendency was reinforced by the infusion of British long-horned cattle that had been imported into the United States at various times. In 1817 some of them were taken to Kentucky, and early Anglo Texans like the Mr. Neal mentioned above may have brought a number of these cattle with them. In 1821 a herd of British long-horned cattle was seen in Ohio.

The colors of the British longhorns were similar to those of many of the later Texas Longhorns—red, red roan, blue roan, yellow, and fawn color. Some had white on the back or belly.[5]

Whether or not British longhorns contributed to the development of the Texas stock, other British breeds did mix with the wild Spanish cattle to produce the Texas Longhorn of the post–Civil War era.

Texas Longhorns might be any of a great variety of colors and combinations of colors, most of them dull rather than bright. There were browns and blacks, solid or with white patches. Whites might be clear or peppered with red (sabinas). Pale red was common, and so were various shades of yellow and dun. Many were pintos, and some duns had dark lines down the back. Brindles and blue or red roans were also frequent. Although the Longhorn became a recognizable breed, it had not existed long enough for any one or two colors to become predominant through superior qualities for survival.

Despite its accidental creation and its ungainly appearance, the old Texas Longhorn was a unique, history-making animal, in this regard unrivaled by any other breed. The long-legged Longhorn was accustomed to ranging far for feed and water. This quality, together with its especially hard hoofs, made the Longhorn ideal for the long drive. The Longhorns' ability to gain weight on the way to market, and the fact that they stayed together and were less likely to scatter than other breeds, also enhanced their value as trail animals. Although they attained their maximum weight more slowly than others, in the days of free grass and open range that was not a serious flaw. With the coming of barbed wire and fenced pastures, however, it quickly became a factor that had to be considered.

On the trail Longhorns fell into position in the herd according to strength or other qualities, and maintained the same place day after day. The strongest cattle were always in the van; the weak or lame were always in the drag. A steer that was lame for several days would fall back into the drag, then resume its former place when its lameness ended.

A few steers instinctively assumed the role of leaders; others followed them without hesitation. When crossing rivers and at other times of trouble good lead steers were as valuable as extra cowboys. Lead steers such as Charles Goodnight's old Blue were so valuable they were used dozens of times and never sold. On

Holding herd on Sherman Ranch, Genessee, Kansas, 1902. The cattle are Longhorns crossed with Herefords and Durhams. Courtesy of the Amon Carter Museum of Western Art, Fort Worth

returning to Texas with the remudas and chuck wagons, these steers easily kept up with the cow ponies. Blue was finally retired to Goodnight's Palo Duro ranch, where he lived another twenty years. On the trail Blue and other veteran lead steers would come to the wagon at night for a handout of biscuits. Blue wore a bell that one of the men tied at night to prevent it from ringing.

In the morning Blue approached one of the point men so he could untie the bell.

Old Tom was another much traveled lead steer. He was large and his horns spread seven feet—each had a gold ring on it near the tip, rings that grateful cowboys had fashioned out of twenty-dollar gold pieces. Old Tom was a proud, natural leader; the cowboys could yell "gee" or "haw" to him, and he would turn in the right direction.[6]

In 1870, Bill Blocker had gathered a herd on the Pedernales when he saw a big, wild bay steer that caught his eye because it looked so proud and free. Blocker's herd was already set, but he decided the bay steer must join it. The steer was soon accustomed to the trail, and it assumed the lead. After ten days Blocker could ride alongside Pardner, as he named the steer, and rest a hand on one of its horns. Sad to say, Blocker was unable to take it back to Texas—this was its only trip up the trail.

Jack Potter's herd in West Texas was saved during a severe blizzard by his lead steer, "John Chisum." While other cattle drifted before the storm, "John Chisum" headed into it, for that was the way to Trempero Canyon and shelter. They came to a fork in a canyon; in the blinding snow Potter took the wrong fork. The steer refused to follow him, so he followed it, and soon was thankful that he had. The herd was saved, while thousands of cattle that had drifted before the storm were lost.

Longhorns reveled in their freedom, and many an old mossy horn bull or steer roped in the brush and yoked to an ox would lie down and die rather than enter a corral. Some became troublemakers on the trail, for they were ever restless and eager to escape, and their nervousness kept the other cattle jumpy and ready to run.

Ben Borroum of Del Rio was taking a herd north one spring; once across the Red River the lead steer began to sniff the wind as Longhorns did when there were buffalo in the vicinity. Soon all of the cattle were nervous, and when bedded down at night they did not let the air out of their lungs as they did when they intended to stay down. The herd ran twenty-two times that night, and no one got any sleep. The next morning a band of Comanches rode up and asked for a "wohaw." Borroum had a couple of cowboys rope the lead steer and take him away from the herd. Once that steer was gone there were no more runs the rest of the drive.[7]

One herd on the Goodnight-Loving Trail stampeded when a night guard's horse caught its hoof in the tree of a McClellan saddle, and the frightened animals ran over the chuck wagon and flattened it. They ran every night after that. John Chisum, who owned the herd and was riding with another of his herds ahead of it, came back after the cattle were bedded down. While riding slowly through the herd he pointed out a leggy, one-eyed pinto steer and ordered the cowboys to separate it from the herd and kill it. There were no more stampedes.[8]

Wherever they went, Longhorns made their presence felt. In 1876, either pranksters or idiots at Fort Benton, Montana, put a Longhorn steer aboard the steamer *Carroll* as a milk cow. Justifiably offended, the steer cleared the decks with a few sweeps of its horns, then "majestically walked on shore and solemnly devoured a quarter acre of *primolo adorato*. No milk on board the *Carroll* this trip."[9]

In 1883, J. L. Hill was with a herd of yearlings and two-year-olds near the North Platte. In the herd was a pot-bellied little dogie that had stayed in the drag all the way from Llano County. The cowboys named it Baby Mine. The trail passed around a rocky bluff overhanging the river; at one place it was so narrow the cattle had to go in single file. One of the larger steers hooked Baby Mine and knocked him over the bluff, sending him sliding down the rock to a fall of forty feet into the water. The drag rider, knowing he would miss the little dogie, said "Goodbye, Baby." But next morning Baby Mine was in his usual place at the end of the herd.[10]

"As trail cattle," Charles Goodnight said of the Longhorns, "their equal has never been known. Their hoofs are superior to those of any other cattle. They can go farther without water and endure more suffering than others."[11] Their meat was marbled, even on a diet of grass, and their hides were more valuable for leather than other cowhides.

Longhorns were also immune to the tick fever that was fatal to other cattle, and the epidemics that followed importations of

Longhorns were the main reason for the bias against them. Once they had been wintered in the North, however, they were free of the disease-carrying ticks.

Of the millions of Longhorns trailed north, less than 40 percent were shipped out immediately. Many were bought by feed lot operators; others were sold to fill beef contracts at Indian agencies. Probably the greatest number went to the new ranches opening all over the northern plains. Steers were held there for a year or two, then sold for beef, having gained several hundred pounds more than they would have gained in Texas. Longhorns fattened better on grass than Shorthorns or other beef cattle, but did not do as well as others on corn. Since corn-fed beef brought the highest prices, cowmen began buying Shorthorn, Hereford, or Angus bulls to cross with Longhorn cows. Such crosses produced excellent range cattle, for they retained enough of the Longhorns' hardiness and ability to forage while acquiring the rapid growth qualities of the other breeds. By the mid-1880s the Longhorn was disappearing from the northern ranges and even Texas. In 1885, D. W. Hinkle wrote Joseph Nimmo that "there are but few, very few, of the old long-horn Texans in the State. All show that good blood has been infused in them."[12]

The Longhorn, which had helped Texas rise from its economic nadir after the Civil War, seemed doomed to early and undeserved extinction as ranchers turned to the British breeds that reached maximum weight quickly. Frank Collinson, who followed many a Longhorn up the trail, wrote the most touching requiem to the vanishing breed.

"Some folks," he said, "pity the bull in the ring at Spanish or Mexican bullfights. I pitied the old Texas Longhorns that came to such a sad end, after weathering the trail so nobly. In my mind they were the real sports. They were among the wildest known cattle and made good beef. They also made good work animals and helped haul heavy loads across the Plains. They could get along without water longer than any other cattle. They had harder and better hoofs. I'm sorry that they are gone from the range."[13]

As a postscript to Collinson's remarks, in the 1920s Texan

Graves Peeler made a search for pure Longhorns and put together a small herd, barely in time to save the breed from total extinction. As the numbers gradually increased, the Texas Longhorn Breeders Association of America was established, and it created a Longhorn registry. By 1978 the association had more than five hundred members and its registry listed upwards of fifteen thousand Longhorns. Because of the qualities that made it valuable a century ago, the Longhorn is again making an impact on the beef cattle industry, and today it has a bright future as well as an illustrious past.

The Longhorn's counterpart in the trailing era was the mustang cow pony. As western writer Eugene Manlove Rhodes remarked to Harry Sinclair Drago, "The mustang and the Longhorn went together like ham and eggs."[14] Together the Longhorn and mustang gave character to a historic era; it would have been a vastly different story without them.

Early visitors to Texas had much to say about mustangs, not all of it in admiration. In 1832, Charles Sealsfield bought one on his visit to Texas. "These mustangs are small horses," he wrote,

rarely above fourteen hands high, and are descended from the Spanish breed introduced by the original conquerors of the country. During the three centuries that have elapsed since the conquest of Mexico, they have increased and multiplied to an extraordinary extent and are to be found in vast droves in the Texas prairies, although they are now beginning to be somewhat scarcer. They are taken with the *lasso*. . . .

The lasso is usually from twenty to thirty feet long, very flexible, and composed of strips of twisted ox-hide. One end is fastened to the saddle, and the other, which forms a running noose, held in the hand of the hunter who thus equipped rides out into the prairie. When he discovers a troop of wild horses, he maneuvers to get to the windward of them and then to approach as near as possible. If he is an experienced hand, the horses seldom escape him, and as soon as he is within twenty or thirty feet of them, he throws the noose with unerring aim over the neck of the one he has

Mounting a bronc, probably a mustang cross. The horse had been ridden before; otherwise the cowboy would have blindfolded it. Photo by F. H. Corbin. The Montana Historical Society

selected for his prey. This done, he turns his own horse sharp round, gives him the spur, and gallops away, dragging his unfortunate captive after him breathless. . . . After a few yards, the mustang falls headlong to the ground and lies motionless and almost lifeless, sometimes badly hurt and disabled.

The breaking process was equally rough on the mustangs, for they were of little value. "The eyes of the unfortunate animal are covered with a bandage, and a tremendous bit, a pound weight or more, clapped into his mouth; the horse breaker puts on a pair of spurs six inches long and with rowels like penknives, and jumping on his back urges him to his very utmost speed. If the horse tries to rear or turns restive, one pull, and not a very hard one either, at the instrument of torture they call a bit is sufficient to tear his mouth to shreds and cause the blood to flow in streams."

The mustang was forced to run until exhausted, then was rested for a time and ridden hard again. "If he breaks down during this rude trial, he is either knocked on the head or driven away as useless; but if he holds out, he is marked with a hot iron and left to graze on the prairie. Henceforward, there is no particular difficulty in catching him when wanted. The wildness of the horse is completely punished out of him, but for it is substituted the most confirmed vice and malice that it is possible to conceive. These mustangs are unquestionably the most deceitful and spiteful of the equine race. They seem to be perpetually looking out for an opportunity of playing their master a trick, and very soon after I got possession of mine, I was nearly paying for him in a way that I had not calculated upon."

When Sealsfield rode near some mustangs on Neal's ranch, his own decided to join them. It ran away with him, then pitched him over its head. Sealsfield's experience on this occasion was one of the reasons for his low opinion of mustangs.[15]

Despite Sealsfield's dislike of mustangs, his contemporary, Colonel H. C. Brish, considered them superior to any others for cavalry mounts.[16] Many mustangs that were well treated by their owners became thoroughly dependable one-man horses.

Josiah Gregg, who traded with New Mexico and Chihuahua in the 1840s, also described the horses. "The New Mexicans," he wrote, "so justly celebrated for skillful horsemanship . . . leave the propagation of their horses exclusively to chance; converting their best and handsomest studs into saddle horses.

"The race of *horses* is identical with that which is found running wild on the prairies, familiarly known by the name of *mustang*. Although generally very small, they are quick, active, and spirited; and were they not commonly so much injured in the breaking they would perhaps be as hardy and long-lived as any other race in existence. Some of their *caballos de silla*, or saddle-horses, are so remarkably well trained, that they will stop suddenly upon the slightest check, charge up against a wall without shrinking, and even attempt to clamber up its sides."[17]

In 1849, W. Steinert, a German visitor to Texas, noted that American horses cost from $100 to $130. What he called pure Spanish horses were priced about the same, and were raised on ranches in Mexico. "The Mexican horse, which is very hardy and can make out on ordinary feed, can be bought for ten, twenty, thirty dollars or more," he wrote. "The mustangs cannot be used much because they rarely become entirely tame. You can buy them for five to ten dollars, but as a rule they run off if they have not been thoroughly trained. Catching and taming them is breakneck work, and it is performed mostly by Mexicans."[18] The Mexican horse Steinert mentioned was the same animal as the mustang except that it had been ranch-raised rather than caught from among wild herds.

Wherever cattle were raised there were also horse ranches, though many ranchers raised their own cow ponies. In 1847 Thomas A. Dwyer established a horse and mule ranch on the lower Nueces, crossing mustang mares with blooded stallions and jacks. "I well remember," he wrote, "seeing thousands and tens of thousands of wild horses running in immense herds all over the western country as far as the eye or telescope could sweep the horizon." The whole country seemed alive with them. He often had trouble controlling his pack mules, for the playful mustangs would keep circling around them on the run and gradually close in, then with a rush make off with the mules. "The supplies of wild cattle and horses then seemed so abundant as to be inexhaustible."[19] Many travelers reported that mustangs had circled them. Trail hands often had to drive them off to keep them from charging through herds and scattering the cattle.

In the 1880s Frederic Remington described the Texas cow pony as having "fine deer-like legs," a long body with a pronounced roach just forward of the coupling, and quite likely a "glass eye" and a pinto hide. "Any old cowboy will point him out as the only creature suitable for his purposes." Though difficult to break and small in size, "he can cover leagues of his native plains, bearing a disproportionately large man, with an ease to himself and his rider which is little short of miraculous."

One thing was certain, Remington added: "Of all the

monuments which the Spaniard has left to glorify his reign in America there will be none more worthy than his horse." Broncos had no equal in intelligence or stamina. "As a saddle animal the bronco has no superior," Remington concluded.[20]

The mustang cow pony, like the Longhorn, had a number of qualities that compensated for others it lacked, such as size and weight. Mustangs had "cow sense," hardiness, endurance, a remarkably good sense of direction, and a wild animal's alertness for signs of danger. In size they were only fourteen hands at best, and they weighed no more than nine hundred pounds on the average. They were adaptable and versatile, serving as roping, cutting, and night horses on ranches, and were used by the Pony Express, the Texas Rangers, and the U.S. Cavalry.[21]

The mustang may have been the original pitching or bucking horse, for pitching is believed to be an American horse trait. There has been much speculation about its origins; the most likely theory is that pumas or panthers, which attack their prey by springing on them slightly behind the shoulders, caused the animals to pitch in an effort to save themselves.[22]

Unlike cattle, wild horses never left their own familiar range voluntarily, for no matter how long and hard they were pursued, they always circled back to it. This trait made it possible for mustangers to "walk down" herds of mustangs by following them constantly in relays. A party of mustangers with access to a corral would camp on the mustangs' range. One man at a time would ride after the frightened animals and keep them in sight until his relief spelled him.

At first sight of a rider the mustangs were off and running, and they might travel sixty miles before turning back. By the third day of constant pursuit with no chance to rest or eat, they allowed the rider to approach fairly near. After a week or ten days the mustangs could be mixed with a tame herd or driven into a corral. Some mustangers attached long rawhide straps to a front leg of each animal just above the hoof, then turned them out of the corral. When they tried to run, they stepped on the strap with a hind hoof and threw themselves. Soon they were easily herded.

Frequently there were domesticated horses or mules run-

ning with the mustangs, and these, having only recently acquired their freedom, were more jealous of it than the mustangs.
Mules were especially alert for the sight or smell of men, and
when one or more of them were with a bunch of mustangs, that
bunch was especially difficult to corral. It was impossible to slip
up close to mules, and when attempts were made to walk them
down, they proved inexhaustible.

On the prairies the strongest and best stallions retained
most of the mares in their harems, though they had to fight off
other stallions, especially during the mating season. Because of
this the mustangs were by no means degenerate. The best of
them made exceptional cow ponies despite their small size.
Among the Mexicans small horses were preferred; their saying
went "Praise the tall but saddle the small."[23]

In the 1860s there was little demand for horses in Kansas, so
the trail hands drove the remudas back down the trail. When
ranching spread in the North, however, northern cowmen soon
realized that they needed both Texans and mustangs to handle
their Longhorns. Thereafter remudas were sold at the end of
the drives, and in addition an estimated million horses, mainly
mustangs, were driven north and sold.

Many of the best cow ponies and cutting horses had formerly been wild mustangs. Some also became winners on the
race track. In 1873, Miguel Antonio Otero, who lived near the
Kansas-Colorado border, bought a two-year-old blue roan stallion from a party of New Mexico mustangers. He gelded the
roan and named him Kiowa. Otero kept Kiowa for thirty years,
during which time he never saw his equal for intelligence, speed,
or stamina. He won many short races, one against a Thoroughbred stallion for one thousand dollars.[24] Sam Bass's Denton
Mare was also said to have been caught by mustangers from a
wild herd.

The mustangs' alertness, sense of direction, and cow sense
made them valuable as night horses, for in a stampede at night
about all a cowboy could do was give his cow pony its head and
hang on. The well-trained night horses found their way over
rough country on the darkest nights as they ran to overtake the
lead steers.

There were many stories reflecting the intelligence of night horses. Some knew exactly when the two hours of night herding were over and would insist on returning to the wagon. Pinnacle Jake Snyder had an old black horse in his string he used for night herding, for it was gentle, wise, sure-footed in the dark, and it liked to work around cattle. He named it Dick Head after the Texas trail boss who sold it to him.

Even on the darkest nights, when Jake had no idea where the chuck wagon was, the horse would stop where he had dropped the picket rope. On one occasion Jake was with a crew driving nine hundred big, wild steers from Porcupine Creek, Wyoming, to Lusk for shipping to Chicago. The country was especially hilly, and it was necessary to bed the steers where other herds had been bedded recently, which added to their nervousness. When one of the relief riders was on his way to the herd, his horse stumbled, his saddle creaked, and the steers were on their feet and running.

Jake had already ridden the ten to midnight guard, but when he heard the familiar rumble of stampeding cattle he ran to his night horse, which met him at the end of the picket rope. Racing after the steers in rough, unfamiliar country was hazardous, and it was a long time before the cattle stopped running. Jake wearily dismounted, leaned against a rock, and slept. Some time later his horse pushed him roughly and woke him up. Jake hastily mounted and the horse was off on the run. Only then Jake learned that the cattle were drifting away and scattering. He managed to hold them together until morning.

During the morning the trail boss rode up, for he had followed the tracks. If Jake hadn't been on the best night horse, he told him, he would have gone over a bank and broken his neck—if he rode over the same country by daylight and saw how close he had come to death his hair would turn white. The strenuous chase after the cattle had used up the old horse beyond recovery. Jake turned him loose on the range and never rode him again.[25]

As ranching spread to West Texas and over the plains, ranchers considered mustangs a nuisance, for they ran off brood mares. When the big ranches were fenced, many mustangs were shot. At the same time mustangers were active, and most of the best mustangs were caught.

Thoroughbred stallions had been introduced into Texas in the 1830s, primarily for racing, but some of these as well as Morgan stallions were bred to native mares to produce fine saddle horses and cow ponies. Most of the racing, at least that which was advertised in the newspapers, was over mile tracks. In 1839, Sam Houston brought the famous Quarter Horse stallion Copper Bottom from Pennsylvania to Texas. In 1840 the first recorded quarter-mile race in Texas was held in Houston, although quarter-mile match races undoubtedly had been held before Anglos arrived in Texas.[26]

Other noted Quarter Horse stallions brought to Texas from Kentucky, Illinois, and Tennessee were Steel Dust, Monmouth, Shiloh, Dan Tucker, and Peter McCue. Many modern bloodlines trace back to them.

By the 1880s the best of the mustangs were gone from the prairies, and mustang blood, like that of the Longhorn, was rapidly being bred out of existence. In Texas the crosses were with Thoroughbreds, Morgans, and Quarter Horses. In the mountainous cattle regions of the North and Northwest larger horses were needed, and mustang mares were crossed with heavier stallions. In Oregon, Clydesdales were popular, and produced a useful, short-set, compact, and muscular horse with large bones and hairy legs—the "Oregon Lummox." In Montana and the Dakotas, Percheron stallions were widely used—their cross on mustang mares was the "Percheron Puddin-Foot." Since the range cattle to be handled were no longer wild and swift Texas Longhorns, the mustangs' speed and endurance were not as necessary as before.[27]

Some of the mustang and mustang-cross cow ponies were exceptional in many ways. Edgar Beecher Bronson, who in 1877 was the first to establish a ranch along the White River in the heart of Sioux country, rode one, the best cow pony he ever owned, to Cheyenne late in September. The horse was a dark red bay, short-backed and deep-barreled, with great blazing eyes and as alert as its mustang ancestors. Its favorite gait was a swift, daisy-clipping lope.

Before he set out on the 121-mile return trip to his ranch, Bronson learned that Dull Knife and the Northern Cheyennes had made their desperate effort to return to the North. Early that afternoon Bronson reached the last ranch between Cheyenne and his own, fifty miles north of Cheyenne. He had planned to spend the night there, but reports that a Cheyenne scouting party had been seen east of the ranch convinced him that travel by daylight was unsafe. He headed on that night, and shortly before sunup reached his own ranch. Between sun and sun his remarkable cow pony had covered 121 miles without quirt or spur.[28]

The mustang and Longhorn were contemporaries of the trailing era, and it is not surprising that when one disappeared the other soon followed. Although the Longhorn has made a rapid comeback since the 1920s, the mustang revival is more recent and not so far advanced, but it has begun. A mustang registry has been established, and the hardy little horses are being bred once more.

CHAPTER 8

The Trail Towns

"Everyone is aware of the amount of money
spent in this city by cattlemen and cowboys."

Fort Worth Democrat

BEFORE the Civil War, Baxter Springs, Kansas, and Sedalia, Missouri, had a brief reign as the principal end-of-trail towns. Both exhibited some of the rough characteristics of the later Kansas cowtowns, but they did not handle large numbers of huge herds and hundreds of trail hands like those that reached Abilene after 1867.

Abilene became a trail town overnight, but its decline was equally rapid. It began as an Overland Stage station which received rare but favorable notice in 1859 when Horace Greeley announced that it was there he ate the last square meal on his trip across the plains. That, and the fact that Abilene had a biblical name, were its sole claims to distinction. In 1867, when Joseph McCoy stopped there in his search for a suitable railhead for Texas cattle, he found only a dozen families living in simple cabins, a post office, a store, and a saloon or two. On September 5 of that year the first trainload of Texas cattle was shipped to Chicago from McCoy's pens.

That first season 35,000 cattle reached Abilene; the following year around 75,000 head arrived; in 1869 the number rose to 160,000. Not all were shipped to market, for many were sold to ranchers in Nebraska. By that time some of the regular residents of Abilene were concerned over the saloons, gambling houses, and dance halls that lined Texas Street. Their efforts to clean up the town were frustrated by the fact that peace officers had a short tenure when the boisterous trail hands were in town. When the Texans saw a stone jail being erected, they happily tore it down.

In 1870, Marshal Tom Smith tamed Abilene somewhat by

122

Ellsworth, Kansas, 1870s. Part of the Drovers Cottage was moved there from Abilene. Western History Collections, University of Oklahoma Library

posting an ordinance against carrying guns. Because Smith enforced the law with his fists rather than with guns, he gained some grudging respect from trail hands before he was murdered while helping the sheriff arrest a couple of killers.

Joseph McCoy, who had brought prosperity to Abilene, purchased cattle on credit in 1869 and lost heavily when the market fell. When the railroad reneged on its agreement to pay him one-eighth of the freight he processed to be shipped from Abilene, McCoy lost everything, even though the courts eventually ruled in his favor. He was able to pay off his debts and he remained closely connected with the cattle business, but he was never again a big operator.

Abilene became famous all over the West, so well known it was natural that people would suppose that it was a city of substance and size. A Texan rode into the center of the town and asked how far it was to Abilene. When told he was there, he replied, "Now, look here, stranger, you don't mean this here little scatterin trick is Abilene." He was told it was. "Well I'll swar I never seed such a little town have such a mighty big name." More important than its size, Abilene's cattle business produced three million dollars a year.[1]

Opposition to the sinful activities on Texas Street intensified, and the permanent residents insisted that the fleshpots be moved to the Devil's Addition outside of town. The saloons along Texas Street remained, and dissatisfaction continued to grow.

In 1870, Abilene had some five hundred residents—the transients who were after the cowboy trade vanished with the last herd of the season and returned before the first herds arrived in the spring. By the trailing season of 1871 Abilene was thoroughly prepared, with ten saloons, five general stores, two hotels, and two so-called hotels in which patrons did not necessarily spend the entire night. The Drover's Cottage, which McCoy no longer owned, catered to trail bosses and cattle buyers; cowboys stayed at the Merchant's Hotel. The men who drove most of the six hundred thousand cattle north swarmed into Abilene in such numbers the saloonkeepers, gamblers, and pimps rejoiced, but the rest of the people had seen enough of Texas cattle and their keepers.

That year was Abilene's most active, but it was also its last year as a trail town. By summer the Atchison, Topeka, and Santa Fe had extended its rails to Newton, near the Chisholm Trail south of Abilene. When the railroad brought Joseph McCoy there to supervise the building of loading pens, a collection of rude shacks was hastily erected. By mid-August 1871 the first trainload of cattle was shipped from Newton to Kansas City. Around forty thousand cattle passed through Newton that year, but its career as a trail town was short as well as violent. By 1873 its trailing days were over, for the Wichita and Southwestern Railroad had reached Wichita.

Early in 1872, before herds had started north, a circular printed in Abilene by the Farmers Protective Association of Dickinson County was circulated widely in Texas. It stated that members of the association "most respectfully request all who have contemplated driving cattle to Abilene the coming season to seek some other point for shipping, as the inhabitants of Dickinson will no longer submit to the evils of the trade."[2] McCoy and others launched a countercampaign to persuade Texans to bring their cattle to Abilene, but in vain.

The Kansas and Pacific Railroad, which had treated Abilene rather cavalierly and had actually tried to cheat McCoy, suddenly awakened to the fact that it was losing the lucrative cattle-hauling business to the rival Santa Fe Railroad. It decided to provide Texans a new railhead that was easily accessible and without the irritations they had suffered from the farmers surrounding Abilene. The new shipping point was Ellsworth, about seventy miles west of Abilene. The railroad hired Shanghai Pierce and Colonel W. E. Hunter to supervise the building of pens, and sent men to mark out a route from the Chisholm Trail to Ellsworth.[3]

The railroad also sent Shanghai Pierce to Texas to persuade cattlemen to send their herds to the new shipping point. With both Newton and Ellsworth offering inducements to trail men, Abilene was ignored. Many Abilene businessmen quickly loaded their wares on wagons, said good-by to deserted Texas Street, and headed for Ellsworth. The new owner of the Drover's Cottage even moved part of it to the new railhead. For a time Abilene was little more than a ghost town, but it soon became the center of a prosperous wheat-growing business. A stone marker was all that reminded people of the town's former days as "Abilene—The End of the Chisholm Trail."[4]

Ellsworth was an instant success as a trail town, for it took over much of the enormous trade that had previously gone to Abilene. From the start it could truthfully claim to be the leading cattle market of Kansas. In its first season, 1872, at least one hundred thousand cattle reached Ellsworth.

Aware of Abilene's troubles with lawlessness, Ellsworth established a police force and confined the "soiled dove" population to the Smoky Hill bottoms outside the town, a district soon known as Nauchville.[5] The police force concentrated on the town proper, leaving Nauchville wide open. Ellsworth's efforts to control violence were no more successful than those of other trail towns. Its police force proved corrupt and adept at cheating Texas cowboys with false arrests and illegal fines. Some men feared that the Texans' resentment would result in an uncontrollable eruption.

John Montgomery, editor of the *Reporter*, tried to avoid the impending blowup by suggesting raising money by licensing the "fair Cyprians" of Nauchville. "If it can't be rooted out," he

Dodge City's Cow-boy Band, which helped publicize the "Cowboy Capital." Courtesy of the Amon Carter Museum of Western Art, Fort Worth

wrote, "the vicious vocation should be made to contribute to the expense of maintaining law and order." Although respectable citizens were shocked at this suggestion, the town council agreed to it,[6] and the licenses provided Ellsworth's main source of revenue.

Ellsworth lasted only a few years as a railhead for Texas cattle, for competition among railroads resulted in the establishment of newer and more convenient outlets. Ellsworth's only big year was 1873, but when the financial panic began in September there were many herds in the area awaiting buyers who never came. Of the thousands of cattle that had to be wintered there that year, fewer than twenty thousand "made it through to grass." No herds arrived in 1874.

The extension of the Santa Fe's subsidiary line, the Wichita and Southwestern, to Wichita in 1872 brought four hundred thousand Texas cattle to that town in 1873. Joseph McCoy had completed the shipping pens in time for the 1872 season. It was at Wichita that the buying of cattle for the northern Indian reservations reached its peak. When the Wichita market opened, some of the merchants who had deserted Abilene for Ellsworth loaded their wagons once more and headed for the new cattle center.

By 1873 Wichita was clearly the major cattle market in Kansas. The town enlarged its shipping pens and built a toll bridge across the Arkansas at Douglas Avenue, which was also designated as the official route for driving cattle through town to the stockyards and shipping pens. Most of the dance halls and saloons were located in the quarter called Delano across the river from the rest of the town, but around the intersection of Douglas Avenue and Main Street saloons and brothels were plentiful.

Wichita had been the northern terminus of Jesse Chisholm's wagon road, for his trading post was near where the town was later built. As a result, in the years of Wichita's preeminence as a trail town—1872–76—the herds followed the original Chisholm Trail a greater distance than at any other time.

Those who bought cattle at Wichita or elsewhere were of three main categories: ranchers from the area from Colorado to the Dakotas in search of stock cattle, feed lot owners from corn belt states, and packing house agents who were after fat cattle. During Wichita's years as a trail town, cattle prices reached their highest level for the whole trailing era. A nine-hundred-pound steer that sold for eleven to fourteen dollars in Texas brought twenty to twenty-five dollars in Kansas, and ten dollars more in Chicago or St. Louis. The same animal might net seventy dollars or more in New York City.[7]

When Tobe Odem sold his herd at Dodge City in the spring of 1877, he told his cowboys their pay would continue until they got back to Goliad with their horses and the lead steer, Old Tom. When they reached Goliad, another herd would be ready. Then he invited them to town for "some fun and few drinks." Dodge City's reputation for wickedness, young cowboy Jesse Benton decided, was undeserved.

"Dodge City were a sight to see: saloons, gambling houses, dance halls on every corner," Benton remembered. There were

Front Street, Dodge City, 1875. Left of center is the Long Branch saloon. Courtesy of the Amon Carter Museum of Western Art, Fort Worth

around five hundred cowboys and buffalo hunters in town, "everybody there to have a good time and blow off from the long trail. I've read some of the most exaggerated things about Dodge City. But they are wrong." Most of the cowboys were good-hearted young fellows with money to spend; if they didn't have any, their boss would furnish it. And, he added, Dodge City knew how to treat them right.

"I walked up to the dance halls and looked in. What a sight to anyone, the prettiest gals from all over the world, dressed like a million dollars, was all there. If you did not come in to dance, they would grab you and pull you in, whether you wanted to dance or not. All the girls acted glad to see you. Round after round of drinks, then all would dance."

Odem bought all the drinks for his men; they didn't return to camp until daybreak. After breakfast they rolled up in their blankets, for no one thought of starting for Texas that day. The following day they didn't feel much better.[8]

By 1876 farms and fences had virtually cut off access to Wichita, and cowmen turned to Dodge City, which had handled some trail cattle from 1872 on. Dodge City would continue to be

Rath and Wright's buffalo hide yard, Dodge City, 1874. Charles Rath sits on a pile said to contain forty thousand hides. Courtesy of the Amon Carter Museum of Western Art, Fort Worth

a major cattle center to 1885–86, the longest existence of any of the Kansas trail towns. This "Queen of the cowtowns," this "wickedest little city in America," this "Beautiful Bibulous Babylon of the Frontier" boasted a saloon for every fifty residents. Perhaps Dodge's earlier history as a center for buffalo hunters and shipping point for buffalo hides had a lasting influence on its character. The other Kansas trail towns all started full-blown as cowtowns.

Because of the profitable hide-shipping business, Dodge largely ignored the possibilities of handling cattle until 1875, although some herds had passed that way as early as 1872, when the Santa Fe tracks reached Dodge. Since there were no loading facilities, herds to be shipped were driven on to Great Bend or elsewhere.[9]

For nearly fifteen years Dodge City was considered the wildest town in the West. By 1875 cattle were regularly trailed there, and it was on its way to becoming the "Cowboy Capital" of the nation. Dodge continued to flourish until 1886, when the quarantines against Texas cattle put an end to the declining trailing business. In its heyday Dodge was the location of the original Boot Hill cemetery, resting place for dozens of men who died with their boots on. It also boasted the Cowboy Band, which helped publicize the city.

The continued spread of farmers and barbed wire pressed a greater and greater percentage of trail cattle on Dodge, but in the end the herds stopped coming. The 1884 quarantine law, which prohibited Texas cattle from crossing Kansas between March 1 and December 1, meant that any herds moving north thereafter would have to keep west of the Kansas line. Many herds made it through in 1884, but none did after that. Kansas cattle were still trailed to Dodge for shipment, but after the big freeze of 1886–87 the Cowboy Capital could no longer be considered an important cattle market.

The last of the Kansas cowtowns to figure prominently in the trailing era was Caldwell, the "Border Queen" on the Chisholm Trail just north of Indian Territory. Caldwell was settled in 1871, but it had no railroad. During the winter of 1873–74, however, when thousands of cattle had to be wintered on the plains, many herds were held near Caldwell, and it served as a supply center and also as the place cowboys went for a spree.

Even before the railroad reached it in 1880 Caldwell already had a reputation for violence and killings. The sight of a horse thief "idling his time away under a cottonwood tree" (at the end of a rope) was not unusual.[10] A marshal's term in office in Caldwell was about two weeks on the average. There was a saying, "In Caldwell you're lucky to be alive."[11]

When the railroad reached Caldwell, it gave the Chisholm Trail a slight but temporary advantage over the Western Trail to Dodge City, but the rapidly spreading farms were making it increasingly difficult to move herds without trouble with grangers, and 1884 was the Chisholm Trail's last year.

As the demand for stocker cattle or young steers blossomed in the North, most of the herds sold in Kansas were delivered to ranches in Wyoming, Montana, or the Dakotas. Ogallala, Nebraska, rose as a new cattle center, and many herds not sold in Kansas found buyers among cowmen assembled there. By the mid-1870s Cheyenne, Wyoming, was another important cattle center where many Texas herds were sold. Ogallala and

Dodge City in 1878. Left of the Billiard Hall is the Dodge House.
Courtesy of the Amon Carter Museum of Western Art, Fort Worth

Cheyenne became as important to Texas cattlemen as the Kansas railheads had been. Cheyenne was, in addition, headquarters for all the cattlemen of the North and Northwest. In 1877, Miles City, Montana, became the cattle center for that region.

The town that benefited most and longest from the Chisholm Trail was Fort Worth. In 1865, as a result of the exodus caused by the Civil War, Fort Worth had more houses than people, for the inhabitants of all ages numbered no more than 250. The empty town made, as newcomer K. M. Van Zandt remarked, "a gloomy picture." The town had a blacksmith shop, a flour mill, and a cobbler's shop, but lacked such vital institutions as a post office and a saloon.[12] As the Longhorn was the economic salvation of Texas, the Chisholm Trail was the savior of Fort Worth, which owed its favorable location on the cattle trail to accident. At least in the early days it was the last place for making purchases before reaching central Kansas.

Before its revival Fort Worth was not impressive. "We went by Waco, Cleburne, and Fort Worth," George Saunders wrote of his first trip up the trail. "Between the last named places the country was somewhat level and untimbered. . . . When we reached Fort Worth we crossed the Trinity River under the bluff, where the present street car line to the stockyards crosses the river. Fort Worth was then but a very small place, consisting of only a few stores, and there was only one house in that part of town where the stockyards are now located. We held our herd here two days.[13]

Other men on the early drives noted that Fort Worth was a small village with few stores, but as the purchases of supplies for trail herds infused new life into the town, the population doubled between 1865 and 1868. It continued to grow because of rumors that a railroad line would soon be extended there.

When Colonel John Wien Forney visited Texas in 1871, Fort Worth's population had grown to upwards of twelve hundred. It was, Forney noted, beautifully situated on a broad plateau. "Fort Worth is a city set on a hill, and as the point of junction between two branches of the Texas and Pacific, is particularly enviable, inasmuch as from this locality the Grand Trunk line to the Pacific will be projected and pushed. . . . During the last year 500,000 head of cattle were driven through Fort Worth on their way to Missouri and Kansas, and as we left the town we met a single drove containing 1250 head."[14]

In anticipation of the coming of the railroad others flocked to Fort Worth, doubling the population again in 1873. Around four hundred thousand cattle had been trailed to Kansas that year, but the financial panic beginning in September left thousands of cattle unsold. What hurt Fort Worth even more was that railroad construction everywhere was suspended. The city's population immediately declined to about one thousand, and "grass literally grew in the streets. This was not a metaphor to indicate stagnation, but a doleful fact" said the editor of the *Democrat*.[15] Former Fort Worth lawyer Robert E. Gowart informed the *Dallas Herald* that Fort Worth was such a drowsy place he saw a panther asleep in the street near the courthouse. To Dallasites, Fort Worth was thereafter Panther City.

Like Abilene's city fathers, Fort Worth officials had to cope with the problems caused by overly exuberant cowboys as well as gamblers, pimps, and prostitutes. In 1873 they passed a number of ordinances prohibiting gambling, prostitution, and the wearing of guns. Because it was soon clear that these regulations were harmful to business, however, the orders were suspended and Fort Worth was again known as a "tolerant" town.[16]

Most of the gambling dens and dance halls were confined to Hell's Half Acre around the intersection of Rusk (later Commerce) and Twelfth streets, and in this district Fort Worth was considered wide open. Like other trail towns that attracted lawless elements, Fort Worth needed some fearless man to keep the peace, and for a time Marshal "Long Hair" Jim Courtright filled the job effectively. When he was hired, his duties were made explicit—he was to keep the peace, not clean up the town.

In 1876, Fort Worth residents turned out, boy and man, to complete construction of the Texas and Pacific track to the city limits. The first train reached the city on July 19, and the expected boom began. By January 1877 all dwellings were filled and an estimated one thousand people lived in tents around the city limits. Fort Worth residents, now confident of their city's future, happily named everything "Panther."

Although some cattle were shipped out of Texas by the various railroads, such shipments posed no immediate threat to the trailing business. It was still far less expensive to trail cattle to Kansas than to ship them by rail.

In 1878, Fort Worth launched a cleaning-up program, and word soon spread among cowboys that a visit to the town likely meant a stopover in the jail. Trail crews now shunned it. In April citizens and businessmen placed an ad in the *Fort Worth Democrat* calling attention to the cost of strict enforcement of laws against drinking, gambling, and other cowboy amusements.

"The cattle season beginning, we think more freedom ought to be allowed as everyone is aware of the amount of money spent in this city by cattlemen and cowboys, thus making every trade and business prosper. We notice especially this year that contrary to their usual custom, almost all of them remain in their camps a few miles from the city and give as the cause the stringent enforcement of the law closing all places of amusement that attract them."[17]

The city council yielded to public pressure, to the great dissatisfaction of Marshal Courtright. As merchants recovered their trade with trail men, the *Democrat* noted that the dance halls were "in full blast again."[18]

By 1880, when the Missouri-Kansas-Texas Railroad reached Fort Worth, the town had a population of 6,663. A year and a half later the Santa Fe also laid tracks through the town, so it had ample rail facilities for serving as a trade and cattle center. It was evident that the city needed to expand its economic base, for the Chisholm Trail would eventually be obliterated by the spread of farms and the increasing use of barbed wire by ranchers.

Former Confederate captain B. B. Paddock, who began editing the *Fort Worth Democrat* in 1872, constantly prodded local businessmen into promoting the city and chided them mercilessly when they let opportunities pass. In the spring of 1875 he had written: "This city is on the nearest and best route. . . . Fencing will be a serious obstacle to herdsmen in many places. This route also allows owners and herdsmen a better opportunity of securing supplies than is afforded by any other route."[19] By 1875 cattle buyers were already coming to Fort Worth to contract for herds moving up the Chisholm Trail.

Looking ahead to the day when the northern trails would be closed, Paddock predicted that Fort Worth would become a center for the meat-packing industry. He chastised the Texas and Pacific Railroad and others for making no effort to develop the shipping of live cattle by offering reasonable freight rates. He pointed out that to ship two thousand head, or one hundred carloads, of cattle from Dallas to St. Louis cost $11,500. The same herd could be driven to Ellsworth, Kansas, for only $1,000; and it cost only $7,500 more to ship them from Ellsworth to St. Louis—a total of $8,500, or $3,000 less than shipping directly from Texas. Eventually the railroads would begin to compete for the cattle business by lowering their freight charges.

Fort Worth continued to grow. In 1877 construction began on the courthouse and the three-story El Paso Hotel, and a slaughterhouse shipped its first carload of refrigerated beef to St. Louis in March. Even though some herds were following the new Western Trail by way of Fort Griffin to Dodge City, many still came up the Chisholm Trail, and the owners bought provisions and equipment at Forth Worth. The cowboys kept the Tivoli Hall, Trinity Saloon, and the various dance halls busy. That same year the Texas and Pacific Railroad shipped more than fifty-one thousand live cattle from Fort Worth.[20]

Although herds continued to pass through or near Fort Worth in the spring of 1878, many turned off the Chisholm Trail at Belton, owing to the blandishments of agents the Fort Griffin merchants sent there to persuade trail bosses to use the Western Trail. Paddock repriminded Forth Worth merchants for supinely allowing so much business to be siphoned off by rivals from Fort Griffin. "That our merchants should have lost sight of the importance of having a representative to offset the influence of Fort Griffin's enterprise at Belton," he wrote "is singular indeed."

When it was known that only 100,000 cattle had followed the Chisholm Trail, while 150,000 had taken the route past Fort Griffin, Paddock renewed his attack: "Had our businessmen been equally active in securing this immense drive, the season drive would not have fallen short of 200,000. Experience is a dear teacher. We hope that their eyes will be opened to their best interest next year."[21] The Fort Worth merchants responded by sending their own agent to Belton to persuade trail bosses to stay on the Chisholm Trail. This effort succeeded, for by late June of 1879 more than 135,000 cattle had passed by Fort Worth, while a little over 100,000 had gone up the Western Trail.

By the early 1880s trailing cattle to or through Kansas was

becoming so difficult that Texas cowmen launched a campaign to have a national cattle trail set aside from Texas to Montana. Northern ranches were now well stocked, and northern cowmen refused to encourage competition from Texas. The project was never approved.

Because of cordial relations already existing between the businessmen of Fort Worth and the cattlemen of northern and western Texas, "Cow Town" remained a cowmen's headquarters even after the Chisholm Trail was only a memory. As the trailing era ended, the railroads began competing for the cattle traffic, and Fort Worth's position as a rail center enabled it to continue to play an important role in the beef cattle business. This role was enhanced by the coming of the packing houses.

In April 1875 the editor of the *Fort Worth Democrat* had written, "There is no reason why Fort Worth should not become the great cattle center of Texas, where both buyer and seller meet for the transaction of an immense business in Texas beef. Fort Worth promises every advantage required in doing a very heavy beef packing business. With an abundance of pure water, ample herding grounds and soon to have shipping facilities by rail to all markets of the East and North, it would seem an admirable point for packing beef."

It was not until 1890, when the Fort Worth Dressed Meat and Packing Company was established, that this advice was followed. In the next few years Swift and Armour opened packing plants in the city. These plants and the business they brought were at least partly responsible for the city's increase in population from around twenty-seven thousand in 1900 to more than seventy-three thousand in 1910.[22]

Trail towns had profited from the trailing business for from several years to a decade or longer. Some declined drastically in population when the herds stopped coming. Although this often meant a distinct improvement in the quality of the local citizenry, it also meant a substantial loss of income. In the more forward-looking or fortunate towns, like Wichita and Fort Worth, other economic activities were quickly developed, and these towns continued to grow on the foundations the trailing era had provided.

CHAPTER 9

Trailing Contractors and Ranching Syndicates

"When everybody is wanting to sell, I buy;
when everybody is wanting to buy, I sell."
George W. Littlefield

WHEN the Chisholm Trail opened, many ranchers had a few
hundred steers to sell but no way to get them to market; those
who had several thousand could not afford to take their cowboys
away from ranch work for several months. All were short of
funds. Almost immediately, however, men devised ways to
gather herds and get them to Abilene without a large cash outlay. A number of arrangements and combinations of plans were
made to the mutual profit of cattle raisers and those who delivered their beeves to market.

One method was payment of a flat fee of $1.00 or $1.50 a
head to a contractor who delivered the cattle and sold them for
the owners. In this case the owners retained title to the cattle and
took the risks, but they also stood to profit when the price was
high. For his fee the contractor furnished crew, cook, wagon,
trail boss, provisions, and horses. This saved the ranchers not
only substantial cash outlays before their cattle were sold but also
responsibility for organizing and conducting the drive. Cattle
lost on the way were charged to the contractor, who naturally
encouraged strays to join his herds. In some cases cattlemen
provided for the expenses of the drive and paid the contractor a
smaller fee.

The contract-trailing business, with its promise of fair
profits with small risks or larger profits with greater risks, attracted many men. So important was their role in moving cattle
to market that in any given year trailing contractors were in
charge of the vast majority of the herds on the trail. Contractors

137

made whatever arrangements the circumstances permitted. George W. Littlefield bought cattle on credit for others, a special type of contracting.

Some, like Dillard R. Fant of Goliad, devoted themselves exclusively to trailing cattle for others; over the years Fant handled about two hundred thousand head. Others, like John T. Lytle, were primarily trailing contractors but also purchased cattle for speculation when conditions seemed promising. In this way they made a guaranteed profit and occasionally added to it substantially when the market was favorable. Lytle and his partners—McDaniel, Schreiner, and Light—were among the major trailing contractors, handling around six hundred thousand head, or perhaps 15 percent of all the cattle trailed out of Texas.

Family firms were also successful trailing contractors, among them George Webb Slaughter and his six sons, Coggins and Parks Cattle Company, Blocker Brothers, Pryor Brothers, Snyder Brothers, and several others. Slaughter began in 1868 by trailing his own marketable beeves and training his sons. In less than a decade the Slaughters trailed and sold cattle worth nearly half a million dollars. Moses and Samuel Coggins had run small ranches before the Civil War, but in 1868 went into the cattle business seriously. They raised and trailed their own cattle and contracted to deliver others for their neighbors. By 1873 they were able to purchase all of the cattle they took to market, thereby greatly increasing their potential profits. They were especially active in stocking new ranches from New Mexico to Montana, and in obtaining government contracts for supplying beef to Indian reservations.[1]

Blocker Brothers of Blanco County was another successful family firm of trailing contractors and ranchers, although two of the four brothers—Ab and Jenks—remained employees rather than partners. At the outset the Blockers delivered cattle for others; thereafter they secured orders from northern buyers and then purchased Texas cattle to fill them. As this business grew they hired W. H. Jennings to buy cattle for them, then made him a partner.

Before their trailing business became so large they had to

hire a number of crews, the Snyder brothers were their own trail bosses. They began by buying cattle on credit and trailing them to Abilene. Over the years Snyder cattle were driven to New Mexico, Colorado, Nebraska, Wyoming, and Montana, where they helped stock the ranches springing up over the northern grasslands.

Another successful family firm was Pryor Brothers Cattle Company of Mason County. Ike T. Pryor drove his first herd all the way to Ogallala in 1876. It was made up of 1,250 steers under contract and 250 of his own. By wise use of his profits Pryor became a major trailing contractor by 1880, when he sent 12,000 head up the trail, mainly cattle he had purchased. On those he owned he made a profit of from three to five dollars a head; on those under contract he made at most one or two dollars.

In 1881, Ike Pryor formed a partnership with his brother and expanded the business. In the spring of 1884 they contracted to deliver forty-five thousand head of South Texas Longhorns, which they moved in one enormous drive of fifteen herds. For this major movement of cattle Pryor Brothers hired 15 trail bosses, 15 cooks, and 160 trail hands. They supplied fifteen chuck wagons, and more than one thousand horses.

The huge drive started off badly, for every herd had scattered during the first week. The cattle were rounded up and pushed up the trail, and the overall loss was only 3 percent. For years afterward Pryor received payments for steers bearing his road brand that had mixed with other herds. In the 1884 season Pryor Brothers made a net profit of $130,000, which enabled them to lease enough rangeland in Colorado to fatten twenty thousand head a year. They lost heavily in the winter of 1886–87, but Ike Pryor remained in the cattle business, recovered his losses, and died a millionaire.[2]

Charles Goodnight and others entered the cattle business as trailing contractors, then used their profits to become cattlemen. In 1866, Goodnight and Oliver Loving contracted to supply beeves to Fort Sumner, New Mexico, and pioneered the Goodnight-Loving Trail there. Although Loving died of wounds received from the Comanches, Goodnight established a ranch at

Charles Goodnight, Texas cowman and trail driver. Western History Collections, University of Oklahoma Library

the Bosque Grande on the Pecos. He arranged with John Chisum to deliver cattle to the Bosque Grande at one dollar a head over Texas prices. Chisum lost two entire herds to Indians, but he and Goodnight developed a profitable relationship; Chisum drove cattle to New Mexico, and Goodnight trailed them on to Colorado. They divided the profits, enabling both men to expand their ranching activities.[3]

As the trailing business expanded, the contractors' methods became more systematic. The Slaughters and Blockers could rely on family members to manage herds and supervise sales. All of the brothers served as trail bosses at first, but when either firm had a dozen or more herds on the trail it was necessary for each brother to oversee a number of outfits at once. Blocker Brothers handled an impressive share of the trail cattle, between three hundred thousand and five hundred thousand, or 7 to 10 percent of all the cattle driven north from Texas. The reason the figures can only be estimated for most trailing contractors is that they kept the barest minimum of records. In the words of Jimmy Skaggs, they were "hip-pocket businessmen."[4]

At the height of the trailing era about a dozen major contractors were responsible for three-fourths of the trail herds. These men were essential to the growth of the cattle industry, for they were the organizers who provided the necessary links between the cattle raisers in Texas and the cattle buyers.

Mark Withers, whose family moved from Missouri to Texas, was one of the most active of the independent trailing men. He made his first drive in 1859 at the age of thirteen, from Lockhart to Fredericksburg, both in Texas. In 1862 he helped trail a herd from Lockhart to Shreveport for the Confederate Army; in 1868, with eight men and a cook, he drove six hundred big steers to Abilene. He bought the steers on credit for ten dollars a head, held them near Abilene to fatten, and sold them in the fall for twenty-five dollars; his expenses were four dollars per steer, which gave him a profit of eleven dollars a head. That same summer Withers took part in Joseph McCoy's wild west show to attract cattle buyers to Abilene. Withers followed the trail from 1868 to 1887, most of the time driving cattle he had purchased.

Another famous Texas trail man was R. G. (Dick) Head, also

from Missouri. At the age of thirteen he helped drive a herd for the Confederate Army, then enlisted three years later. After the war he trailed cattle for Colonel J. J. Myers, and soon had full charge of Myers's trailing business, which meant supervising a dozen herds on the trail at the same time.

In 1875 Head became general manager for Ellison, Dewees, and Bishop, trailing contractors who moved from thirty thousand to fifty thousand cattle a season. Head and Bishop were partners from 1878 to 1883; the next three years Head was general manager for the British-owned Prairie Cattle Company, which operated three large ranches. In 1886 he became president of the International Range Association, and owned an interest in ranches in Texas and New Mexico.

Hundreds of men trailed cattle from Texas during the two decades the trails remained open. Some succeeded and became fairly wealthy; others lost their investments because of troubles with Indians or outlaws, or because of price fluctuations or the lack of buyers. Some men were able to finance the wintering of their herds and were fortunate enough to sell them profitably the following season. Others lost nearly all of their cattle because of severe weather. Among those who trailed cattle for a living, as in other businesses, what counted most was efficiency. Men who had the knowledge and ability to supervise the successful movement of ten or fifteen herds in a season were the ones who became wealthy.

The services the trailing contractors provided were less costly than shipping by railroad by four or five dollars a head, which could mean as much as fifteen thousand dollars more in profits on a single herd. If weather and other conditions were favorable, the cattle usually gained weight on the trail. Cattle shipped by rail, on the other hand, lost weight and frequently were injured.

Trail men estimated that it cost sixty cents a head to move cattle 1,500 miles; a federal survey of 1886 put the figure at seventy-five cents.[5] In 1884 the breakdown of trailing expenses was thirty dollars a month each for nine riders and a cook, and one hundred dollars for a trail boss, for a total of four hundred dollars. Adding one hundred dollars for provisions, the total cost, after the initial outlay for wagons and horses, was five hundred dollars to move three thousand cattle 450 to 500 miles. Until the railroads revised their rate schedules and made them competitive, trailing was much less expensive than shipping. As long as the trails remained open, the trailing contractors played a vital role in the range cattle business.

Another product of the trail drives and the cattle boom was the syndicate, domestic or foreign, that went into the cattle business on a grand scale and provided the funds for rapid expansion. Much of the capital that launched the syndicates came from Britain. A great many Britishers also came to the cattle country, some eager to be cowboys, others determined to become ranchers or ranch managers. John Clay and Murdo Mackenzie, both Scots, were two of the most successful ranch managers. Mackenzie, for years the boss of the Matador, was one of the best-known cowmen in the country.

When easterners and Britons began buying cattle and range rights, ranch managers were in great demand, but only men of superior qualities. Isaac Ellwood, owner of the Frying Pan Ranch, expressed the desires of many: "I want a man who knows something of land and water problems, can make a good bargain in cattle sales and is able to manage cowhands." He was advised to settle for someone "who can get along with your men and is reasonably honest. If you receive this he will be worth his pay." As Ellwood advised his son William, "The major success of a ranch, my friends in Texas tell me, is due to its choosing a good manager."[6]

Managing one of the huge ranches was no simple matter. "It was not an easy job," wrote Nebraska cowman John Bratt, "to handle two hundred or more cowboys with nearly a dozen different outfits and one thousand to twelve hundred horses, keeping the work moving intelligently, finding camping places for each outfit and see that all, even the lone representative, had equal share and a square deal, but I had a reputation for doing it."

The main reason for the flurry of investment in ranching syndicates was the widespread delusion about easy wealth to be made in the open range, free grass, cattle industry. Encouraging the expectations of certain and substantial profits that helped spark the wild speculation in cattle in the 1880s was the publication in 1881 of James S. Brisbin's *The Beef Bonanza; or, How to Get Rich on the Plains.* A U.S. general who had served for years on the plains, Brisbin spoke with authority, and he verified the rumors and stories of fabulous profits to be made that had circulated throughout the East and in Britain.

Emphasizing the relative decline in cattle breeding, Brisbin concluded that "for at least ten years yet the stock growers need have no fear of overstocking the beef markets."[7] It was, according to Brisbin, ridiculously easy to sit back and let one's profits accumulate on free grass and open range. To raise a three-year-old steer worth twenty-five to thirty dollars cost only six to ten dollars. Hundreds of investors leaped at the opportunity; few of them ever saw a return on their money. And while it may have been true that there was no immediate fear of glutting the market, there was a real danger of overstocking the range.

Even before Brisbin's book appeared many easterners had invested in western range cattle companies. All no doubt expected to make handsome profits, but there were plenty of other get-rich-quick schemes available. Many were intrigued by the reports of friends who had already bought stock in some cattle company; others had already put money into western mining or railroad ventures. For a time investing in the range cattle business was considered smart.

Until the main influx of eastern and British capital, the partnership was the usual type of large ranch organization. Easterners such as banker Augustus Kountze and his brothers might enter an agreement, or "association," with a western cattleman such as Shanghai Pierce of South Texas. In 1885 the Kountzes agreed to furnish the capital to purchase two hundred thousand acres and twelve thousand yearlings selected by Pierce, who would receive one-sixth of the profits from cattle sales. Although relations between the conservative Kountzes and the colorful Pierce were stormy, the arrangement proved profitable to all concerned.[8] Other easterners entered similar agreements with individual cowmen, but not always with happy results.

Like the Kountze-Pierce partnership, most of these were

marred by misunderstandings caused by unreasonably high expectations on the one hand, and a growing irritation with those who provided the funds on the other. Often the eastern partners, totally unfamiliar with the cattle ranges, tried to lay down conditions that could only outrage the cowmen. James T. Gardner of Albany, New York, for example, wrote his partner, George McClellan, "Be sure to hire sober men; I shudder at the thought of our cattle running around the plains cared for by some fuzzy minded cowboy."[9] As more and more investors turned to the beef cattle business, the partnership was superseded by the syndicate, with its board of directors and multitude of stockholders.

One of the major difficulties of syndicate ranching was maintaining satisfactory communications between managers and their employers, for neither understood or appreciated the problems of the other. Some managers wrote infrequently and told their distant superiors as little as possible; others wrote lengthy, rambling letters. Neither practice was what was desired, but, as one manager glumly noted, they were damned for whatever they did or didn't do.

Managers also prepared annual reports, presumably to keep stockholders informed on range conditions and prospects for sales. The manager's annual report was almost a new branch of American literature, if semifiction could be considered new, for it was skillfully written to beguile and please far-off directors and shareholders. Bad news was artfully disguised or omitted. Managers did what they believed was expected of them; it seemed clear they were called on to produce good news. After the cattle boom collapsed, annual reports became dull and factual, for shareholders wanted no more double talk or fairy tales.[10]

Syndicate ranches, especially foreign-owned ones, experienced labor troubles that had not been characteristic of cowman-cowboy relations in the past. The basic problem was that the average cowboy could not respect absentee owners, especially British aristocrats who looked on cowboys as their retainers and, when they visited their ranches, expected a show of deference and humility.

Typical of the incidents resulting from this attitude, which provoked deep resentment among cowboys, was the Englishman Moreton Frewen's visit to one of the Wyoming ranches in which he had invested. Ranch manager Hank Devoe met him as he rode up; Frewen handed him the reins and ordered him to unsaddle his horse. Devoe informed him that he was nobody's servant.

"I own an interest in this ranch and I will have you fired," Frewen told him. Devoe replied that he couldn't fire him, for he had already quit.[11]

William A. Baillie-Grohman had a warning for other Englishmen who planned to run ranches in the West: "It is 'to do as others do.' That marked feature of America, social equality, which, while it has often a way of expressing itself in a very extravagant and disagreeable fashion, is undoubtedly a main factor in the unusually rapid growth of the Great West, must never be forgotten by the English settler. A man out West is a man, and let him be the poorest cowboy he will assert his right of perfect equality with the best of the land, betraying a stubbornness it is vain and unwise to combat. This is an old truth. . . . In connection with the cattle business it is . . . of tenfold importance: in no vocation is popularity more essential than in this, for let a man receive once the name of being possessed by unsociable pride, and there will not be a man in the country who, while he otherwise would gladly share his last pipe of tobacco or cup of coffee with him, will not then be ready and willing to spite or injure him."[12]

Some of the ranches with absentee owners were pilfered by their own employees as well as by their neighbors. It was well known that such ranches had a smaller calf production and many more mavericks than others. Small ranchers resented being virtually crowded off the overstocked ranges, and they didn't hesitate to kill even branded strays from big ranches for food, or to brand any mavericks they found. Some cowboys paid saloon debts or provided for their mistresses by marking calves with their brands or even altering brands. The Sweetwater, Wyoming, ranch that John Clay managed used a 71 (71 quarter circle) brand. The owner of a nearby road ranch and saloon adopted the rocking chair brand (ௗ), which could easily be made out of the ୬ quarter circle.[13]

Although there was occasional hostility between big and small ranchers, some of the big ones treated the small ones fairly and maintained cordial relations with them. During the round-ups these small ranchers were "dinner reps" when the wagon and crew were in their area. They got their cattle rounded up and branded, had a few square meals, and usually carried home a big piece of beef the cook gave them.

Concerning ranch management in the North, Colonel Samuel Gordon of the *Yellowstone Journal* noted later, "As a majority of the 'companies' and individuals knew nothing of the business, it was essential that there be at the head of each outfit a manager or superintendent to take charge of the technical part of it. These managers were usually cowboys who had become 'top-hands' on the southwestern ranges and were absolutely competent to run herds, but were rarely good financial managers."

Some company ranches, he continued, had competent businessmen as managers, men who were out of place on the range. "Looking backward, it is hard to guess which method was most disastrous; the manager with 'cow sense' but no idea of the value of money, or the thrifty financier who didn't know a branding iron from a poker. They were bad combinations, each of them."[14]

Despite the investors' great expectations from their managers, few managers were well paid—ninety dollars a month was probably close to the average. Exceptions were Dick Head of the Prairie Land and Cattle Company, Murdo Mackenzie of the Matador, and John Clay. But most were less fortunate; as one protested to the distant owner, "You expect us to spend nights on the range, using sod as a bed, drinking brackish water, while you enjoy good food and a soft bed, all for the smallest money."[15] Curiously, most investors saw no connection between adequate pay and managerial effectiveness. The managers' only alternative was to ask frequently for loans, which investors dared not refuse or insist on being repaid.

The sudden influx of nesters, or homesteaders, who

preempted some of the best land and cut off access to water, forced all ranchers to buy at least enough land to give them control of the water. Faced with the unexpected need to buy thousands of acres, many investors had to overextend their credit, even though some had never received a single dividend from the money they had invested in cattle. But in order to protect their investments, the big ranches had to buy land; often it meant sending good money after bad. Forced to acquire land for survival, some cattlemen did not hesitate to fence in huge sections of the public domain.

In 1879 fencing became a serious concern in the North as the Swan Land and Cattle Company, the Anglo-American Cattle Company, and other large outfits fenced vast areas of federal or railroad land, in some cases enclosing homesteads as well. Because of complaints, in 1883 the secretary of the interior authorized settlers to destroy illegal fences that blocked their way to land they wanted to homestead. In 1885 Congress outlawed such enclosures of the public domain, and President Cleveland ordered the fences removed.[16]

One of the most successful of the syndicate ranches, the Matador, was established in 1879 and branded its first calf crop 50M, reflecting the fifty-thousand-dollar capitalization. Later this brand was used only on horses. In 1882 Scottish investors bought the Matador, made it a joint-stock company, and increased its holdings to more than a million acres.

Although the Matador's cattle had been purchased according to the customary tally book count, and it paid for many more than it received, under the astute management of Scot Murdo Mackenzie the ranch prospered. At the outset the Matador sold young cattle to northern ranchers, who profited by grazing them for two years and then selling them for beef. In 1892, Mackenzie arranged for Western Ranches to graze two thousand head of Matador two-year-old steers along the Little Missouri. This introduced a new phase of cattle raising that enabled the Matador to profit not only by breeding cattle but also by maturing them in the North and marketing them. The company acquired its own range in Montana; because trailing was still less expensive than shipping by rail, the Matador trailed its own herds north until

1896.[17] Other big ranches in Texas adopted the same practice. The Prairie Land and Cattle Company, the "mother of the British companies," was organized in Edinburgh in 1880–81. The western range cattle industry had been presented to Scottish investors as simply a matter of buying young cattle, fattening them on free grass, and selling them. So obvious a way to wealth attracted investors by the hundreds. The new company bought ranches in Colorado, New Mexico, and Texas. Its early profits, however, especially the first year's sensational dividend of slightly more than 20 percent, were from the sale of recently purchased cattle, not from natural increase.

For a few years during the 1880s there were scores of ranching companies organized on the tenuous foundations of blind faith and great expectations. There was something satisfying about investing in cattle ranches, inviting friends to visit the ranch headquarters, and wining and dining them at the Cheyenne Club. But, as Britisher William A. Baillie-Grohman mourned, "In no business is a man so dependent upon his neighbors, so open to petty annoyances, and so helplessly exposed to vindictive injury to his property as in stock raising out West."[18]

The years 1882, 1883, and 1884 were deceptively successful for the rapidly expanding western range cattle business, for prices remained high and there were plenty of eager buyers. In 1885, however, managers suddenly reported that the ranges were overstocked. When two extraordinarily severe winters followed, the Prairie Company, like most of the others, was hard hit. But although many went out of business, it survived until 1917.[19]

The XIT Ranch was established in 1882 when the Texas legislature offered three million acres in the Panhandle in exchange for building a new capitol (larger than any other state possessed) to replace the one that had burned down. The contract went to the Capitol Syndicate, John V. and Charles B. Farwell and Associates, of Chicago. At its greatest extent the XIT was about two hundred miles long and from twenty to forty miles wide, for the Farwells added fifty thousand acres to the original three million. Ab Blocker, who delivered the ranch's first herd, suggested the XIT brand as one that rustlers could not easily alter. Since the XIT included all or parts of ten counties, to many the brand meant "Ten in Texas."

The Farwells ran the XIT with efficiency and success. They eventually fenced the entire ranch, a job which required six thousand miles of barbed wire. The ranch employed 150 cowboys and ran 150,000 cattle. The Farwells, learning that the northern ranges were superior for fattening cattle, acquired a finishing range of about a million acres in Montana. They trailed young steers to it each year, and ran as many as 30,000 head on their Montana range. By 1906 all of the XIT's indebtedness had been paid off.[20]

John Clay represented Scottish syndicates that owned ranches in California, Wyoming, and Kansas during the peak years of investment in range cattle. In those years, when there were more potential buyers than sellers, cattle were bought on tally book records of roundups and of the number of calves branded rather than on actual range counts of the cattle sold. These book count deals, Clay discovered, were invariably disasters, for the tally books might show twice as many cattle as were actually on the range. But buyers optimistically paid for the book counts; men who insisted on actual counts were ignored as long as there were others less cautious with money to spend. The winter of 1884–85 was severe, and many Wyoming ranchers gloomily discussed their losses in Luke Murrin's saloon in Cheyenne. "Cheer up boys," he told them, "whatever happens the books won't freeze."[21]

Among the cattle kings of Wyoming was Alexander Swan, who began ranching in 1873. With his partner, Joseph Frank, he owned thousands of cattle on a vast range extending from near Ogallala, Nebraska, to Fort Steele, Wyoming, and from the Union Pacific Railroad to the Platte River. The principal Swan range was from the Chug and Sybille creeks westward over the mountains to the Laramie plains. Such an enormous range could make a man feel godlike, and that misfortune befell Alec Swan.

Swan was, nevertheless, a pioneer in the upgrading of Wyoming range cattle. In 1877 he began bringing Hereford bulls from Illinois and Iowa, and in 1883 imported purebred

Hereford cows and bulls from England. As a result of his efforts, in some years Swan cattle sold for twice as much as cattle from other ranches.[22]

When Swan and Frank asked John Clay to make a report on the Swan holdings to be used in organizing the Swan Land and Cattle Company in Scotland in the spring of 1883, Clay refused unless there was to be an actual count of the cattle. The subject was quickly dropped, and Clay's services were not required. Because Swan had a great following of sycophants, investors in his company did not demand a range count of his cattle. Swan was carried away with his own power, and when he fell he dragged his friends and employees down with him; none of those he had helped in the past was willing to lend him a hand. As Clay remarked, "His rise was meteoric, his fall terrific, and in 1887 when he failed, it was the forerunner of many disasters."[23] Swan's failure shook the whole range cattle industry to its very foundations. In March 1888 Clay was named manager of the Swan Company, and he labored for more than eight years to enable the company to survive. Under his management it recovered somewhat, but by 1910 it had sold its cattle and turned to raising sheep.[24]

Among the eastern cattle barons were Harvard classmates Hubert Teschemacher and Fred de Billier, who in the late 1870s bought three ranches in Wyoming. Although they made satisfactory profits in 1881, the division of managerial duties and the poor keeping of financial records jeopardized their success. In 1882, Richard Trimble, another Harvard classmate, joined the firm, increasing the division of management responsibilities. The firm survived the bad winter of 1886–87, but it foundered and failed soon after.[25]

Many cowmen of the northern and central plains were ruined by the winter of 1886–87, since few had shown any foresight and most had overstocked their ranges. Many easterners and Britishers lost all interest in the range cattle business when they discovered that it was by no means an avenue to easy wealth. As John Clay summed it up, "The gains of the open range business were swallowed up by losses. From the inception of the open range business in the West and Northwest from say

1870 to 1888, it is doubtful if a single cent was made if you average up the business as a whole."[26]

Most of the big syndicates that survived the winter of 1886–87 were liquidated between 1900 and 1920, although a few, like the Matador, continued to stay in business. In most cases the emphasis shifted from cattle to sheep, agriculture, land sales, oil leases, or other activities. The tremendous investments in the range cattle business had enabled it to expand rapidly in the 1880s; if the investments had been made on more realistic foundations, it seems unlikely that the era of the big ranches would have ended so quickly.

CHAPTER 10

The Spread and Collapse of the Cattle Kingdom

"The gains of the open range business were swallowed up by losses."

John Clay

THE spread of the cattle kingdom from the Rio Grande to Canada was rapid in the late 1870s and early 1880s, for cattlemen followed in the tracks of the retreating buffalo and plains tribes. A story that was widely circulated at the time concerned freighter E. S. Newman, who in the winter of 1864–65 was caught on the Laramie plains at the onset of winter. He left his oxen to starve, but found them fat when he returned in March. By this incident Newman learned that cattle could not only survive winters on the northern plains but actually gain weight at the same time. The Newman brothers became major cattlemen, with two ranches in Wyoming and others in Nebraska, Indian Territory, and West Texas.[1]

Many men had, in fact, long known that cattle thrived in the region, as the buffalo had before them. As early as 1830 William Sublette, Jedediah Smith, and others had taken a few cattle into the Wind River valley, and three years later Rocky Mountain Fur Company men had brought cattle from Missouri to the Green River rendezvous. In 1843, John C. Frémont saw cattle in the Platte valley of Colorado where the trading post called Fort Lupton was later built. A band of Mormon pioneers introduced the first breeding cattle into Wyoming in 1847, and in 1852 army sutler Seth E. Ward of Fort Laramie wintered hundreds of oxen in the Chugwater valley.[2]

As soon as the Oregon Trail was opened in the 1840s, cattle, both oxen and breeding stock, traveled acrosss the plains to Oregon. In 1849, Richard Grant, formerly of the Hudson's Bay

153

Roundup crew, tents, chuck wagon, and remuda. Tents and cook's awning indicate they were on a northern range. Courtesy of the Amon Carter Museum of Western Art, Fort Worth

Company, began raising cattle at his trading post in the Jefferson valley of Montana. Within a few years other men were bringing cattle to the Bitterroot valley for fattening and sale to settlements along the Columbia River. During the 1850s others brought cattle to the same region as well as to the future site of Missoula.

When Granville Stuart took sixty head to Montana in 1858 he found a number of small herds already there. By 1863, he noted, the cattle industry was well established in the Alder Gulch mining area. As further evidence of the importance of cattle raising, in 1864 Montana's first territorial legislature passed a law regulating marks and brands.[3]

In 1866, Nelson Story went from Montana to North Texas and for ten thousand dollars bought around one thousand cattle, mostly cows with calves thrown in. With twenty-five cowboys he pointed the herd north, overcoming one obstacle after another all the way to Montana. The summer was unusually wet on the plains, and most of the rivers were over their banks. The cattle, Story complained, swam as much as they walked. Toll collectors harrassed him in Indian Territory, and bands of armed men threatened him in Kansas.

When Story and his cattle finally reached Fort Phil Kearny on the Bozeman Trail, Colonel H. B. Carrington ordered them to go no farther. The trail led through the last hunting grounds of the Teton Sioux, and Red Cloud's Oglalas were determined to preserve them against invasion by whites. Story's men were armed with new Remington breech-loading rifles, however; they ignored Carrington's order and continued at night up the trail. They got through with only one brush with the Sioux and the loss of one man. Story kept his breeding stock, bought others, and established a ranch near Bozeman.[4] In 1869, W. D. Jeffers brought one thousand Texas cattle to the Madison valley in a drive that took six months. In the next two years he brought up three thousand more Texas cattle.[5] In 1871 many cattle were trailed from Texas to Montana and settled on ranches in the Sun valley, along the Missouri River, and in the Big Hole country.[6]

Montana's major cattleman was Conrad Kohrs, who got his start by operating butcher shops in mining camps, a job that kept him constantly searching for cattle. In 1866 he bought John Grant's ranch and cattle in the Deer Lodge valley, although the land had not been surveyed and Grant had no title. Kohrs continued building up his herds with Texas Longhorns and Shorthorns from Missouri. Later he brought purebred Hereford bulls to his ranch and experimented with crossbreeding.[7]

John W. Iliff, for a time the leading cattleman of the whole Northwest, arrived at the Cherry Creek mining region of Colorado in 1859, the same year that John Dawson brought a herd to the Cherry Creek camps. Iliff began buying oxen and fattening them to sell as beef to the miners. By 1865 he was fully occupied with raising cattle, and began buying selected parcels of land to obtain control of the limited water supply over a vast range running one hundred miles east and west and upwards of sixty miles north and south. He bought Texas cattle from Charles Goodnight and imported Shorthorn bulls from Illinois and Iowa. By the time of his death in 1878 his land and cattle were worth a million dollars.[8]

Pioneer cattlemen of the Great Plains found the grass exceptionally nutritious. As Iliff noted, "I have engaged in the stock business in Colorado and Wyoming for the past fourteen years. During all that time I have grazed stock in nearly all the valleys of these territories, both summer and winter . . . no feed or shelter is required. I consider the summer-cured grass of these plains and valleys as superior to any hay."[9]

Another early cattleman, R. C. Keith of North Platte, Nebraska, began raising cattle in 1867 with a few "American" cows. In both 1869 and 1870 he bought one thousand Texas cattle. By 1875 he had sold sixty-three thousand dollars' worth of cattle and had a herd of more than five thousand valued at nearly one hundred thousand dollars.[10]

Although many parts of the plains remained unsafe for men and cattle as long as both buffalo and plains warriors roamed freely over them, cattle raising had spread fairly widely along the borders of the Sioux country by the mid-1860s. In the summer of 1865 a Dr. Corey followed the Loup Fork of the Platte northwest of Omaha to the Niobrara and the base of the Black Hills, then returned along the Big Horns and down the

Cowboys on the XIT range, Montana, 1905. Photo by John L. Breum. The Montana Historical Society

Platte. On the way he saw numerous herds of cattle, sheep, and horses. "Old mountaineers, hunters, and trappers all told me," he reported, "that the winter grazing was fine and uninterrupted by snow. I have been familiar with the winter grazing in that country for six winters, and I am sure the stock will winter on the native grass without shelter."[11]

It was not the discovery that the grass supporting millions of buffalo would also support cattle that led to the explosive spread of cattle ranches in the northern and central plains. Until the

virtual extermination of the buffalo in the 1870s, the Sioux, Cheyennes, Comanches, and Kiowas could not be controlled, and men who valued their hair had to wait on buffalo hunters and the U.S. Cavalry. The new military posts on the plains and in the mining camps provided steady markets, and as the buffalo disappeared the thousands of reservation Indians also had to be fed beef.

Even before the great flood of cattle from Texas to Wyoming and Montana began, herds were driven to those regions from Oregon and Utah. Oregon's first cattle were those Ewing Young trailed from California to the Willamette valley in 1836; two years later the Hudson's Bay Company brought in two thousand more over the same route. In 1843 the major migration to Oregon began, and many good-quality "Pilgrim cattle" accompanied the emigrants.[12] Beginning in 1875 some of these cattle were trailed to Wyoming and Montana, where they mixed with Longhorns from Texas. The peak year was 1880, when between 150,000 and 200,000 head were driven out of Oregon. Thereafter Oregon had fewer surplus cattle to export.[13]

Among the early Colorado and Kansas cattlemen, in addition to John Iliff, were Joseph P. Farmer, John Hittson, William K. Schaeffer, and Charles Goodnight. Farmer came from Ireland, arriving in 1861 in Colorado, where he bought land that gave him control of water along the West Bijou, a tributary of the Platte. Starting with a few Texas cattle and Shorthorn bulls, by careful management he built up a herd and, at the same time, a stable of blooded horses.

Hittson had first settled in Palo Pinto County, Texas, and at one time owned one hundred thousand head. But chronic Indian troubles caused him to shift to Colorado, where he bought a half section of land on the middle Bijou that effectively controlled the only available water in that area. In 1873 he drove eleven thousand of his Texas cattle there, and in the following year brought up twenty thousand more.

Schaeffer earned money to become a rancher by trailing a herd of steers from Texas to Nevada. Although the drive lasted a year and a half, he sold the cattle for fifty-two dollars a head in gold, making it a profitable venture. He bought four thousand acres in central Kansas along the Saline River, and used it to winter twenty-five hundred cattle each year. He owned no stock cattle, but bought and fattened Texas steers, making substantial profits and greatly reducing the risk of losses. In a typical year he bought twenty-five hundred steers for twenty dollars a head, or fifty thousand dollars. It cost him two dollars a head to hold them until time to sell, and about ten thousand dollars in interest on his loan. Camp supplies and other items for his men might cost an additional $2,500, making his total investment $67,500. He sold the cattle for $93,750, or a net gain of $26,250.[14]

Charles Goodnight and Oliver Loving were among the first cowmen to drive Texas cattle to New Mexico and Colorado.

After Loving's death, Goodnight turned to ranching rather than trailing; in 1868 he bought rangeland southwest of Pueblo, Colorado, and a few years later acquired another large tract of land near Trinidad. Later he established a ranch in Palo Duro Canyon, Texas.

Although there was an irrepressible delusion that the rangeland and grass of the Great Plains were inexhaustible, as early as 1876 J. M. Wilson of the Colorado Cattle Growers Association expressed doubts. In the January meeting of the association he said, "The belief seems to prevail with those who have not watched and noted its steady decline, that our range is unlimited, and that all that is necessary is to come with horses, cattle and sheep, no matter how many, and turn them loose, and all will do well." Colorado's rangeland was extensive, he admitted, but "that it is unlimited, and cannot be overstocked, is simply nonsense, and the sooner we realize the truth the better for ourselves and the better for the country."[15] It would be only a decade before Wilson was proved to be painfully correct.

In the North there was more conflict between the big spreads and the little ranches than in Texas, although the "Fence War" was largely an attack of small ranchers on large ones. The cattlemen's association that met in Jacksboro, Texas, in 1883, the year the war began, passed a resolution to the effect that the state legislature should enact laws protecting property rights against wanton destruction. All property taxed by the government, the resolution continued, "is entitled to the same protection, no matter to whom belonging, and whether the property be used for agricultural or grazing purposes." And there should be gates wherever public roads passed through the pastures.[16]

South Dakota small rancher Bruce Siberts maintained that there was open hostility between big and small ranches in that region. One of his steers got in with Hash Knife cattle and was shipped with them to Chicago and sold by the Wyoming Stock Growers Association, which put the proceeds from the sale of the steer into its stray account. Even though Siberts presented proof of ownership, he was refused the money.

Later when he accompanied a shipment of cattle to Chicago,

Siberts called on Clay Robinson of the Wyoming association, who told him he would have to bring suit to collect his money. Siberts vowed he would collect it on the range in his own way. Robinson, Siberts recalled, didn't like it and "talked pretty mean to me." He never heard of a little rancher being reimbursed for cows he lost in a big roundup, but he suspected that the policy cost the big ranchers more than they gained. Their cattle were widely scattered, and it was easy to kill strays from distant ranches.[17]

Some ranchers, such as Print Olive and his brothers, brutally eliminated little ranchers in Texas as well as in the North. Wherever the Olives ranged their cattle no small rancher was safe, and many who occupied land the Olives wanted in both Texas and Nebraska disappeared, either driven out or murdered.

The big ranches of Wyoming continued to suffer heavy losses to rustlers. In 1892 a group of frustrated ranchers hired some Texas gunmen and invaded Johnson County to deal justice to some of the more notorious cattle thieves. They were soon outnumbered and surrounded by irate residents of the county; troops from Fort McKinney apprehended the cattlemen and took them to Cheyenne, where they were eventually released. Undoubtedly there was right as well as wrong on both sides. What heightened the conflict in the North was the fact that most of the struggle was for control of lands the federal government owned, not private holdings. In Texas, once barbed wire was accepted, cattlemen large and small quickly acquired title to the land they used or quit ranching. For this reason there was little resentment against Texas ranchers who decided to run sheep as well as cattle on their own lands.

In Wyoming it was partly resentment against easterners and Britons who established huge ranches that stimulated cattle stealing, for it was never more widespread than in that time and area. Edgar Beecher Bronson was one who overcame the Texans' dislike for "No'therners," and was able to hire a loyal crew. "While all the best punchers were Texans," Bronson wrote, "the elders themselves were ex-Confederate soldiers."[18] Even when stock association inspectors arrested men who had stolen cattle in their possession, it was nearly impossible to secure convictions from local juries, whose sympathies were with the "little men." When, for example, a Colorado stock inspector arrested a man who had five Pony Cattle Company calves in his barn, witnesses solemnly testified that it was quite common for calves to leave their mothers and break into barns. The thief was acquitted. The inspector angrily and unwisely remarked that this was what was to be expected when a cow thief jury and a cow thief judge tried a cow thief. The judge heard about the remark and fined him twenty-five dollars.[19]

Since fewer than half of the cattle sent up the trails from Texas were immediately shipped out by rail, the others went to stock new ranches or to Indian agencies, army posts, or feed lots. Credit was vital to the cattle business. Cowmen who could not sell their cattle were obliged to hold them on the range over the winter, which usually meant borrowing money for current expenses. In 1873, for example, when the financial panic drove away potential buyers, Texas cowmen in Kansas borrowed a million and a half dollars. Credit would become increasingly important in the cattle boom of the 1880s. As Gene Gressley has pointed out, the "Western range cattle industry during the last two decades of the nineteenth century was operated basically on borrowed capital."[20]

As new ranches sprang up over the northern plains, Texas cattle, horses, and cowboys were much in demand. Some Texas cowmen also settled in the North, but there was a greater influx from the East and from Britain. No matter where the owners were from, they all soon learned that for handling wild cattle on the open range they needed at least a nucleus of Texans. Early settlers in Montana and the Dakotas remarked that they could not step outside their cabins and spit without hitting a Texan.[21]

As a result, Texas cowboys gave their stamp to the entire range cattle industry east of the Rockies. Their style differed considerably from that of the California vaqueros and the Oregonians who copied it. For a time dally and tie-fast roping styles mingled in the Northwest, but the tie-fast custom of the more numerous Texas cowboys eventually predominated.

No one questioned the fact that Texans knew cattle and

horses as no other men, but off the range their knowledge was extremely limited before they broadened their experience by going up the trail. Texans were known in the North by the unflattering term of "Rawhides," since rawhide, or "Mexican iron," was the plastic mending or binding material for all things—in this sense the forerunner of baling wire.

Texans referred to men from farming regions as "short-horns," and to non-Texas northern cowboys as "sagebrush men" or "God-damn knock-kneed Oregonians." Teddy Blue Abbott, who settled in Montana before large numbers of Texans arrived, enjoyed telling "Texas" or "Rawhide" jokes about the newcomers.

One reason so many Texans remained in the North after delivering herds to ranchers in Wyoming and elsewhere was that Texas outfits fed their men as cheaply as possible. In the North there were wealthy easterners and Britons who enjoyed being cattle barons. They loved to bring friends to visit their ranches, especially during roundups. They liked to "rough it" with the men, but in comfort and style; the result was that diet and working conditions in the North were vastly superior to what they were in Texas. Even tents and cots were supplied for round-up and trail crews. Although a few old-time Texas cowboys grumbled at such evidence of physical and moral decay, they soon saw the advantages.

Few Texas cowboys had ever seen white flour or sugar in the early days, for cornmeal and sorghum took the places of wheat flour and sugar. A favorite "Rawhide" joke was of a Texas cowboy who rode into a Montana roundup camp at mealtime. When he poured a cup of coffee someone handed him a sugar bowl. "No thanks," he said, "I don't take salt in my coffee."[22]

Texas cattle reached the Cheyenne region as early as 1867 or 1868, and they continued to arrive. By 1874 there were an estimated ninety thousand cattle in Wyoming Territory; six years later the number had increased to more than five hundred thousand. The first beef shipment east from Wyoming was in 1870. A Wyoming stock growers' association was organized at Cheyenne in 1871, six years before the first one was organized in Texas.[23]

The cattle available in Wyoming in the late 1870s were of several grades. Cheapest were the "gaunt, leggy, wild long-horn stock of straight Spanish breed come out of the chapparal along the lower reaches of the Rio Grande; the dearest, the thick-loined, deep-quartered, dark red half-breed short-horn Oregonians, descended from some of the best Missouri and Illinois strains, trailed by emigrants across the plains in the early 50s. Between these two extremes were two intermediate grades, the Middle Texas and Utahs."[24]

Although British syndicates bought up most of the Texas Panhandle, even more Britons flocked to Wyoming, Montana, and the Dakotas, where vast quantities of open range grassland had only recently been opened to occupancy by cattlemen. Wealthy men enjoyed the prestige of owning huge herds and controlling an immense acreage; for many youths, including remittance men, it was glamorous and adventuresome to become cowboys.

Wealthy easterners and eastern college students were also attracted to the cattle country, for popular magazines frequently carried articles on the cattle kingdom and the men who ruled it. Many, like Theodore Roosevelt and Edgar Beecher Bronson, hoped to improve their health in the West.

One of the by-products of this influx of wealthy and educated men from the East and the British Isles was the establishment of the exclusive Cheyenne Club. There was nothing like it elsewhere in the cattle country, which perhaps was fortunate, for the members were more concerned with social graces than with calf crops. As John Clay observed, one might meet men all over the world who "gloried in the fact that they were members of this unique place."[25]

The Cheyenne Club set the social tone for the northern ranchers. Club members wore tuxedos for dinners and soirees; cowboys uncharitably labeled them "Herefords." Some members tried to maintain the same atmosphere at their ranch headquarters. At the Swan Ranch, for example, guests were served champagne at all meals. Ranchers like the Swans dazzled their guests by taking them to the Cheyenne Club. "Here with the flash of youth on their brows in the late seventies and early eighties came Britishers and Bostonians, New Yorkers and Ohians, not forgetting Canucks and Chicagoans, a motley group full of ginger and snap, with more energy than business sense. . . . There was an atmosphere of success among its members. They spent money freely, for all along the line there was a swelling song of victory."[26]

Some Wyoming ranchers were seduced by the Cheyenne Club's high-toned atmosphere and tried to uphold it by maintaining costly establishments in town as well as at ranch headquarters. Well-stocked bars and lavish entertainment did nothing to upgrade herds. Visiting their ranches only occasionally, and accompanied at such times by throngs of admirers, these men invited disaster, and disaster accepted.

The Cheyenne Club was, however, also the business center. Scientist Clarence King stopped at the club on his way to the Pacific coast. By the time he departed he was involved in a partnership with N. R. Davis and in several other cattle schemes. It was to N. R. Davis that Edgar Beecher Bronson went with a letter of introduction from King.

The Cheyenne Club was also headquarters for remittance men from England and wayward eastern scions whose families banished them to the West in hope of "redemption or at least retribution."[27] Owen Wister, when touring the West, called the Cheyenne Club "the pearl of the prairies." But the club was as out of place in the West as some of its misfit members; it gradually lost its glitter and eventually had to close its doors.

The flood of British capital into the cattle industry caused uneasiness throughout the United States. What raised fear and resentment was alien ownership of large tracts of land—by 1883 twenty-one of the major American cattle companies were incorporated in Britain. Scottish investment in the western cattle industry was around twenty-five million dollars; British companies owned or controlled at least twenty million acres of rangeland.

Opposition to this alien invasion was expressed in various state governments as well as in Congress. Governor James Hogg of Texas predicted that the huge British holdings in his state would be divided among "inferior foreign tenants" who would give political power to the aristocratic landlords.[28] States such as

Texas which tried to legislate against alien ownership of property saw their efforts blocked by the courts as unconstitutional. While eastern and British men and capital were heading for Cheyenne or elsewhere in the cattle kingdom, thousands of cattle plodded up the trail toward the same ranges. Men with trail herds were still likely to encounter opposition whenever they exposed local cattle to the ravages of tick fever. In 1869 some Colorado farmers had tried to turn back a Goodnight herd; Goodnight's cattle came from central Texas, however, and they were free of the disease. Apparently the farmers refused to accept Goodnight's explanations. Finally he ran out of patience, loaded his shotgun, and ordered his men to get Winchesters from the chuck wagon. They rode up to the men blocking the herd. "I've monkeyed as long as I want to with you sons of bitches," Goodnight informed them. The roadblock was immediately lifted.[29]

In the 1880s, as all the trails were closed except through the Panhandle, Goodnight and other ranchers of that area established a "Winchester quarantine" of their own against herds from South Texas. Tick fever was the main reason for their action, but they admitted that cattle from other parts of Texas were also competitors.[30]

By 1882 there were signs that even the route to and past Dodge City was closing, for farmers who had settled north of the town were protesting against herds crossing their lands. A year later armed men were demanding payment from trail bosses for allowing their herds to pass through and to use the water holes. Trail bosses had no choice but to pay for water.

In the spring of 1885 the protest was so strong that the Kansas legislature virtually prohibited Texas cattle from crossing the state. Ranchers who had spent money upgrading their cattle were especially opposed to risking devastating losses from tick fever such as had occurred in 1884, one of the worst years.

When word spread that herds moving up from Texas would reach the Canadian River early in June 1885, ranchers' associations met and decided they must fight to protect their cattle. The herds left the old trail at the Texas border and turned west through the Neutral Strip toward Colorado. Cowmen of the

Cherokee Strip and Kansas, as well as some "bad men" from Dodge City, rode south to intercept them. They nervously set up a "war camp" on a creek southwest of Camp Supply, about fifty miles north of the Texas herds along the Canadian.

One morning there was great excitement over a rumor that seventy-five Texans were on their way to wipe out the defenders. All were ready to concede defeat and head north. John Clay and another man agreed to ride south and check on the supposed invasion. At Wolf Creek they came to a line camp, where some cowboys had just returned from visiting the herds and trail crews along the Canadian. They reported that there had been great excitement over rumors that Kansas cowmen were on the way to drive them back into Texas.

There was no battle. The Kansans had a good laugh and went home. John R. Blocker, who had herds on the Canadian, wired Washington, and cavalry troops were detailed to see that the herds got through unmolested. As the Kansans had feared, however, hundreds of their cattle died of tick fever.[31]

Because of the variety of possibilities for calamities such as this, the range cattle business was one in which losses could be staggering. The Snyder brothers, for example, were once among the wealthiest of western cowmen—in 1884 they turned down an offer of one million dollars for their land and cattle. After the severe winter of 1885 they were in debt an equal amount.[32]

In the rapid expansion of the 1880s many ranchers carried heavy debts. One Texan glumly remarked that he was living on "the interest on what I owe." Ike Pryor recalled a South Texas rancher who asked a lawyer to examine his will. The lawyer was surprised that he had named six bankers as pallbearers, and asked if he would not rather have friends in that role. "No, Judge, that's all right," the rancher replied. "Those fellows have carried me so long they might as well finish the job."[33]

One of the signs of impending disaster was the reckless way men invested in cattle raising without knowing anything about it. Don Lovell, Andy Adams's cowman in *The Outlet*, commented in 1884 after seeing a rank amateur mismanaging a trail herd: "Boys, there goes a warning that the days of the trail are numbered. To make a success of any business, a little common sense is necessary. Nine tenths of the investing in cattle today in the Northwest is being done by inexperienced men. No other line of business could prosper in such incompetent hands, and it's foolish to think that cattle companies and individuals, nearly all tenderfeet at the business, can succeed. They may for a time,—there are accidents in every calling,—but when the tide turns, there won't be one man or company in ten survive. I only wish they would as it means life and expansion for the cattle interests in Texas. . . . But there's a day of reckoning ahead, and there's many a cowman in this Northwest country who will never see his money again. Now the government demand is a healthy one; it needs the cattle for Indian and military purposes; but this crazy investment, especially in *she* stuff, I wouldn't risk a dollar in it."[34]

Northern ranch managers consistently wrote optimistic reports to stockholders or owners, playing down winter losses as "probably one or two percent." Experienced cowmen in Montana considered 10 percent a normal annual mortality. After herds purchased on tally book counts had been ranged in the North four or five years, owners were beginning to inquire why beef shipments were not larger.[35]

The year 1885 was the high point of the range cattle industry on the Great Plains, for profits were high and optimism unbounded. Although the Great Plains ranges were already overstocked, in August President Grover Cleveland ordered cattlemen to remove their cattle from the Cheyenne-Arapaho Reservation in Indian Territory. This forced two hundred thousand more cattle onto overcrowded ranges just before winter set in. The winter was severe in the central plains, and by spring 85 percent of these cattle had died.

The summer of 1886 was unusually dry over much of the Great Plains, and there was little grass to be found. Despite this, more and more cattle were driven up from Texas or east from Oregon and Washington onto ranges already overgrazed. In July, South Dakota rancher Theodore Roosevelt commented that well-managed ranches were making fair profits, but there were now too many men in the cattle business, and the day of excessive gains was past. He noted the effects of the drought and of too many cattle, for he had not seen a "green thing" anywhere.

On August 1 the *Glendive Times* of Montana observed that cattle prices were depressed and most cattlemen were reluctant to ship their stock until the market improved, "but the condition of the ranges does not encourage this desire to hold their cattle." The *Helena Independent* added another note of caution in September, because of the lack of moisture and scarcity of grass. It concluded that "much depends upon the coming winter." Observant men saw only ominous signs. The fall rains were light; the remaining beavers piled up unusually large supplies of saplings for their winter food supply. Ducks and geese headed south much earlier than in other years, and range cattle grew longer coats than usual.[36] Snow fell several times in November, and Teddy Blue Abbott saw white arctic owls for the first time. "The Indians said they were a bad sign, heap snow coming, very cold, and they sure hit it right," Abbott recalled.[37]

Heavy snow began falling on Christmas Eve, and it continued to fall off and on for most of the next two months. Late in January the warm breeze called the Chinook melted the snow on the surface; then temperatures plunged below zero. "The snow crusted," said Abbott, "and it was hell without the heat."[38] The blanket of ice over the snow was impenetrable; cattle died by the thousands, many of thirst.

Future cowboy artist Charlie Russell was working on the OH Ranch of Jesse Phelps. When one of his partners wrote Phelps asking about range conditions, Russell drew a humped up, starving cow, calling it "Waiting for a Chinook." Someone changed the title to "The Last of Five Thousand"; it helped launch Russell's career in art. Phelps tore up the letter he was writing and sent only the drawing for a reply.[39] In the spring the Montana Stockgrowers Association summed up the situation as "a drouth without parallel; a market without a bottom; and a winter, the severest ever known in Montana."[40]

Cattlemen were stunned; none could fathom the extent of his losses until the spring roundup, and even then men kept hoping their cows had drifted south before the storms and would show up in some distant roundup. Roosevelt returned to his ranch to determine his losses. "Well," he wrote Henry Cabot Lodge, "we have had a perfect smashup all through the cattle country of the northwest. The losses are crippling. For the first time I have been utterly unable to enjoy a visit to my ranch."[41] As John Clay concluded, "It hit the just and the unjust. It was the protest of nature against greed, mismanagement, and that happy-go-lucky sentiment which permeates frontier life."[42]

In the spring Granville Stuart sent Teddy Blue Abbott as his representative on roundups to the south, but a big drive on Timber Creek netted only one lean steer. The roundup boss sardonically asked all of the reps present if they didn't want to cut the herd for their brands.[43] On one range where there had been forty thousand cattle in the fall, the roundup crew found seven thousand.

In July, Abbott and others were working the range around Box Elder Creek in hot weather and the heavy stench of dead cattle. "There was one old fellow working with us who had some cattle on the range," Abbott recalled later; "I don't remember his name. But I'll never forget the way he stopped, with sweat pouring off his face, and looked up at the sun, sober as a judge, and said: 'Where the hell was you last January?' "[44]

Granville Stuart's losses were reckoned at about 66 percent; others suffered even heavier losses, for of the cattle brought up from the south the previous summer, only 10 percent survived. "A business that had been fascinating to me before," Stuart remarked, "suddenly became distasteful. I wanted no more of it. I never wanted to own again an animal that I could not feed and shelter."[45]

Through the spring of 1887 cattlemen north and south were in a state of gloomy apprehension, and when they finally realized the appalling extent of their losses, some threw up their hands and quit. As early as January the huge Dolores Land and Cattle Company of Texas went under. Even worse news was in store, for in May Swan brothers failed. Since Alec Swan was widely admired and idolized as a financial wizard, news that his company was being reorganized was as shocking as if some deity had announced that his heaven was in receivership.

There is, however, another side to the Big Die-up, as Colonel Samuel Gordon of the *Yellowstone Journal* pointed out many years later. "It is comforting," he wrote, "to reflect on the number of reputations that were saved by the 'hard winter' of 1886–87. It *was* a hard winter—the latter end of it—and the worst of it came when the cattle were weak and thin and unable to stand grief, but it never killed half the cattle that were charged to it. It came as a God-sent deliverance to the managers who had for four or five years past been reporting 'One percent losses,' and they seized the opportunity bravely, and comprehensively charged off in one lump the accumulated mortality of four or five years. Sixty percent loss was the popular estimate. Some had to run it up higher to get even, and it is told of one truthful manager in an adjoining county that he reported a loss of 125%, 50% steers and 75% cows. The actual loss in cattle was probably thirty to fifty percent, according to localities and conditions."[46]

The Big Die-up of 1886–87 did not result in a wholesale exodus of eastern and British capital, as has often been implied, although many men did abandon any connection with the cattle business. Some investors had become unhappy even before the disastrous winter, for it had already become clear that the anticipated easy profits would never materialize. Many investors retained their stock in cattle companies, but new investments were slow to come. Companies with adequate capital and able managers survived and soon recovered. In western Montana ranchers had put up hay for winter feeding for several years, and their losses were much lower than those of central and eastern Montana.[47]

One man who quickly took advantage of the situation was the Frenchman Pierre Wibaux of South Dakota, who had access to funds from France at the time investments from the East and Britain had virtually dried up. In the spring of 1887 Wibaux began buying up remnants of herds at twenty dollars a head. That fall he sold the beeves only, at a profit of forty to forty-five dollars on each animal. He continued buying up entire brands, and by 1890 owned forty thousand cattle and branded ten thousand calves. Because of the shortage of cattle, prices remained high for several years, to the considerable advantage of men like Wibaux who had beeves to sell.[48]

Conrad Kohrs lost heavily in the Big Die-up, but he recovered quickly. He borrowed one hundred thousand dollars and purchased about nine thousand steers in Idaho, all that were available. In 1889 he bought more cattle in Idaho and Oregon, making a profit of fifteen dollars a head. His best year was 1891, when his profits averaged $62.50 a head and total sales amounted to $290,000.[49]

The Big Die-up marked the end of an era by hastening the end of the cattle boom. That phenomenon would have ended in any event because of overstocking, overproduction, and poor management. In coming years quality took precedence over quantity in the cattle business, which meant owning and fencing ranges, upgrading herds, and providing winter forage. The cattle industry recovered fairly quickly, but the day of the open range was not yet over in Montana. "Before the end of the eighties, there were more cattle on Montana ranges than ever."[50]

The problem of overcrowding by cattle and sheep on the eastern Montana ranges again became serious in the 1890s, for the number of ranchers who depended on the public domain for most of their pasture but owned or leased land to produce hay for winter increased considerably after the hard winter. In the 1890s the size of herds in the region declined, as small ranchers gradually replaced the open range cowmen. The damage had been done, however, for the best grasses had been cropped too closely, and in some places had died out, to be replaced by poorer grasses or sagebrush. As Robert S. Fletcher has observed, "Overstocking had become a cruel reality in the last years and a hastening agent in the movement toward a new era."[51]

Whenever cattle prices were low, cowmen usually blamed the meatpackers, whom they viewed as monopolists determined to ruin cattleraisers. The solution seemed to be to fight the packers with their own major weapon—monopoly. Edward M. McGillin of Cleveland, who invested heavily in the range cattle industry, was one of the leaders of the movement. Early in 1887 he presented members of the International Range Association with a plan for a beef trust incorporated at one hundred million dollars.

The purpose of the huge trust was to "arrange, manage, sell every animal from the time it was dropped a calf until it was beef." The American Cattle Trust created in the spring of 1887 was patterned after the Standard Oil Trust. Its board of directors included prominent western cattlemen as well as eastern financiers: R. G. Head of New Mexico, John T. Lytle and C. C. Slaughter of Texas, and Francis E. Warren and Thomas Sturgis of Wyoming. Sturgis was elected chairman of the board.

The American Cattle Trust was launched with enthusiasm and expectations, but it was torn by dissension between eastern and western trustees, and many cattlemen refused to join. In 1889 it was on the verge of bankruptcy, for its efforts to secure markets in the East had been defeated by Swift and Armour. By the summer of 1890 it was no more, but it had taught cattlemen and investors one valuable lesson: their only hope of curbing the meat-packing industry was through political action.[52]

With the end of the range cattle boom, western ranching changed drastically from what it had been in the era of open range and free grass. Genuine cowmen, for whom raising beef cattle was the only acceptable way of life, adapted to the new conditions and continued. Even those who had lost everything could not abandon the life they loved; many swallowed their pride and worked for others on ranges where they had once grazed their own cattle. In a letter to barbed wire maker Isaac Ellwood asking for a job as manager of his Frying Pan Ranch, Dudley Snyder added, "Please don't think for a moment I would feel humiliated in managing your business after having owned the greater part of it."[53]

The cattle kingdom and trailing era lasted little more than twenty years, but in many ways these were the most memorable two decades in the nation's history. Then everything changed. Fenced pastures ended the open range and cut up the trails. The nervous Longhorns, the first truly American cattle, disappeared; placid Herefords, Angus, and other imported breeds that matured quickly, took their places. Muscular Quarter Horses, which had originated in colonial Virginia, displaced the little mustang cow ponies. Trail bosses and their crews had no place in the new order; the cowboys who succeeded them dug post holes, strung wire, and repaired windmills. Cattle cars superseded trail drives. There were no more great open range roundups, no mavericks. Ranchers even learned to eat their own beef.

The passing of the old West was mourned by many, but it was not forgotten. Over the years it has, as C. L. Sonnichsen noted, come to fill our basic need for a "heroic past." We have made the nameless hired men on horseback our Galahads and Gawains, the chuck wagon our Round Table. The old West is still with us, for we need it more than ever.

Notes

INTRODUCTION

1. W. H. Hutchinson, "The Cowboy and Karl Marx," *Pacific Historian* 20 (Summer 1976): 119.

2. Oscar Edward Anderson, Jr., *Refrigeration in America: A History of a New Technology and Its Impact* (Princeton: Princeton University Press, 1953), pp. 47–61; Mary Whately Clarke, *A Century of Cow Business: A History of the Texas and Southwestern Cattle Raisers Association* (Fort Worth: Texas and Southwestern Cattle Raisers Association, 1976), pp. 86–89.

3. Henry D. and Frances T. McCallum, *The Wire That Fenced the West* (Norman: University of Oklahoma Press, 1965), pp. 68–70.

4. Gene M. Gressley, ed., "Harvard Man Out West: The Letters of Richard Trimble, 1882–1887," *Montana, the Magazine of Western History* 10 (Winter 1960): 20n; Wayne Gard, "The Fence-Cutters," *Southwestern Historical Quarterly* 51 (July 1947): 1–15.

5. Richard Irving Dodge, *Our Wild Indians: Thirty-three Years' Personal Experience among the Red Men of the Great West* (Hartford: A. D. Worthington and Co., 1886), pp. 608–9.

6. Wayne Gard, "Retracing the Chisholm Trail," *Southwestern Historical Quarterly* 60 (July 1956): 61; John R. Lunsford, "E. B. Baggett Speaks of Chisholm Trail," *Frontier Times* 8 (December 1930): 127.

7. Gard, "Retracing the Chisholm Trail," p. 55; Richard Harding Davis, *The West from a Car-Window* (New York: Harper and Brothers, 1892), p. 136.

8. W. J. Morris, "Over the Old Chisholm Trail," *Frontier Times* 2 (April 1925): 41–43. Morris was actually describing the Western Trail to Dodge City. Charles Moreau Harger, in "Cattle-Trails of the Prairies," *Scribner's Magazine* 11 (June 1892): 734, states that the Chisholm Trail was named for John Chisholm, "an eccentric frontier stockman, the first to drive a herd over it."

9. Gard, "Retracing the Chisholm Trail," p. 53; Wayne Gard, *The Chisholm Trail* (Norman: University of Oklahoma Press, 1954), p. vi.

10. C. L. Sonnichsen, *From Hopalong to Hud* (College Station: Texas A & M Press, 1978), pp. 8, 16–18. See also Joe B. Frantz and Julian Ernest Choate, Jr., *The American Cowboy: The Myth and the Reality*

(Norman: University of Oklahoma Press, 1955), and William W. Savage, Jr., "The Cowboy Myth," *Red River Valley Historical Review* 2 (Spring 1975): 162–71. Reflecting the universal interest in the American West are the Westerners International corrals of Norway, Sweden, West Germany, Denmark, France, Britain, Japan, and Mexico.

Chapter i

1. Gilbert J. Jordan, Jr., tr. and ed., "W. Steinert's View of Texas in 1849," pt.5, *Southwestern Historical Quarterly* 81 (July 1977): 46. See also "The First Cattle Ranch in Texas," *Frontier Times* 13 (March 1936): 304–8.

2. Rupert Norval Richardson, *The Frontier of Northwest Texas, 1846 to 1876* (Glendale, Calif.; Arthur H. Clark Co., 1963), p. 155.

3. Michael Doran, "Antebellum Cattle Herding in the Indian Territory," *Geographical Review* 66 (January 1976): 48–54.

4. Grant M. and Herbert O. Brayer, *American Cattle Trails, 1540–1900* (Bayside, N.Y.: Western Range Cattle Industry Study in Cooperation with the American Pioneer Trails Society, 1952), p. 28.

5. In 1832, when Charles Sealsfield visited Neal's ranch, Neal was preparing to drive twenty or thirty steers to New Orleans.

6. J. Frank Dobie, "Tom Candy Ponting's Drive of Texas Cattle to Illinois," *Cattleman* 35 (January 1949): 34–55; George Squires Herrington, "An Early Cattle Drive from Texas to Illinois," *Southwestern Historical Quarterly* 55 (October 1951): 267–69.

7. Joseph G. McCoy, *Historic Sketches of the Cattle Trade of the West and Southwest* (Columbus, Ohio: Long's College Book Co., 1951), p. 88; Thomas Ulvan Taylor, *The Chisholm Trail and Other Routes* (San Antonio: Naylor Co., 1936), pp. 4, 7–9.

8. Richardson, *Frontier of Northwest Texas,* p. 253.

9. Ibid., pp. 262–63.

10. Ramon Adams, *The Best of the American Cowboy* (Norman: University of Oklahoma Press, 1957), p. 138.

11. Will S. James, *27 Years a Maverick; or, Life on a Texas Range* (Austin: Steck-Vaughn Co., 1968), p. 67.

12. Ibid., p. 73.

13. Ibid., pp. 74–76.

14. Michael S. Kennedy, ed., *Cowboys and Cattlemen* (New York: Hastings House, 1964), pp. 103–8.

15. William Curry Holden, *A Ranching Saga: The Lives of William Electious Halsell and Ewing Halsell,* 2 vols. (San Antonio: Trinity Univer-

sity Press, 1976), 1:63; Taylor, *The Chisholm Trail,* pp. 90, 98.

16. Louis Pelzer, *The Cattleman's Frontier: A Record of the Trans-Mississippi Cattle Industry from Oxen Trains to Packing Companies, 1850–1890* (Glendale, Calif.: Arthur H. Clark Co., 1936), pp. 38–40.

17. McCoy, *Historic Sketches,* p. 102. The following direct quotation is from the same source, p. 65.

18. Holden, *A Ranching Saga,* p. 64. See also, E. P. Earhart, "Up the Cattle Trail in 1867," *Frontier Times* 8 (February 1931): 194–95.

19. McCoy, *Historic Sketches,* pp. 185–88.

CHAPTER 2

1. Ernest Staples Osgood, *The Day of the Cattleman* (Minneapolis: University of Minnesota Press, 1954), p. 29.

2. J. Frank Dobie, *A Vaquero of the Brush Country* (New York: Grosset and Dunlap, 1929), pp. 198–99.

3. E. C. ("Teddy Blue") Abbott and Helena Huntington Smith, *We Pointed Them North* (Norman: University of Oklahoma Press, 1954), p. 61.

4. Richardson, *Frontier of Northwest Texas,* pp. 153–263.

5. See Clarke, *A Century of the Cow Business;* Lewis Nordyke, *Great Roundup: The Story of the Texas and Southwestern Cowmen* (New York: Morrow, 1955); and "Old Cowman Tells of a Big Steal," *Frontier Times* 3 (June 1926): 36–37.

6. McCoy, *Historic Sketches,* p. 145.

7. Ibid., p. 146.

8. Orland L. Sims, *Cowpokes, Nesters, and So Forth* (Austin: Encino Press, 1970), p. 58.

9. Emily Jones Shelton, "Lizzie Johnson: A Cattle Queen of Texas," *Southwestern Historical Quarterly* 50 (April 1947): 349–60.

10. Gene M. Gressley, *Bankers and Cattlemen* (Lincoln: University of Nebraska Press, 1966), pp. 174–77.

11. Joyce Gibson Roach, *The Cowgirls* (Houston: Cordovan Corporation, 1977).

CHAPTER 3

1. W. J. Morris, "Over the Old Chisholm Trail, p. 42.

2. Abbott and Smith, *We Pointed Them North,* p. 62.

3. James G. Bell, "A Log of the Texas-California Cattle Trail, 1854," ed. J. Evetts Haley *Southwestern Historical Quarterly* 35 (April 1932): 304.

4. Dobie, *Vaquero*, pp. 91–92.

5. Ibid., p. 93; Jesse James Benton, *Cow by the Tail* (Boston: Houghton Mifflin Co., 1943), p. 45.

6. Andy Adams, *The Log of a Cowboy: A Narrative of the Old Trail Days* (Lincoln: University of Nebraska Press, 1964), p. 231.

7. Abbott and Smith, *We Pointed Them North*, p. 67.

8. Gard, *The Chisholm Trail*, p. 243.

9. J. Frank Dobie, *The Longhorns* (Boston: Little, Brown Co., 1941), p. 97.

10. Taylor, *The Chisholm Trail*, pp. 181–82; J. Marvin Hunter, ed., *The Trail Drivers of Texas*, 2 vols. (New York: Argosy-Antiquarian, 1963), 2: 636.

11. Dobie, *Vaquero*, p. 262.

12. Dobie, *The Longhorns*, p. 111; Abbott and Smith, *We Pointed Them North*, p. 83.

13. Ibid., p. 68.

14. Benton, *Cow by the Tail*, pp. 4–49.

15. Ibid., pp. 49–53.

16. Hunter, *Trail Drivers*, 1:67; Jack Potter, "Up the Trail (and Back) in '82," *Montana, the Magazine of Western History* 11 (October 1961): 64.

17. Abbott and Smith, *We Pointed Them North*, p. 62. The following quotation from Jesse Benton is from *Cow by the Tail*, p. 70.

18. James, *27 Years a Maverick*, pp. 89–90.

19. Ibid., p. 91.

20. Benton, *Cow by the Tail*, pp. 69–70.

21. Randolph B. Marcy, *The Prairie Traveler* (Williamstown, Mass.: Corner House Publishers, 1968), pp. 118–20.

22. Ramon Adams, *The Old Time Cowhand* (New York: Macmillan Co., 1961), p. 105.

23. Sims, *Cowpokes*, p. 48; Will James, *Lone Cowboy* (New York: Charles Scribner's Sons, 1930), p. 178; Fred Fellows, "Illustrated Study of Western Saddles," *Montana, the Magazine of Western History* 16 (January 1966): 57–83.

24. Jane Pattie, "The Justin Boot: Standard of the West," *Quarter Horse Journal* 29 (September 1977): 127; "The Justin Boot," *Montana, the Magazine of Western History* 11 (January 1961): 86.

25. Walt Coburn, *Pioneer Cattleman in Montana: The Story of the Circle C. Ranch* (Norman: University of Oklahoma Press, 1968), p. 130. Stetson hats were available in the West at least by 1871. Levis were shipped to Texas soon after the Civil War. Bull Durham tobacco and

cigarette papers were also available about the same time. Foster-Harris, *The Look of the Old West* (New York: Bonanza Books, 1955), pp. 105, 112–13, 204.

26. Coburn, *Pioneer Cattleman,* p. 137. The term *cowpuncher* seems to have originated at the railroad loading chutes, where men prodded cattle with long poles. The term was used mainly in the North.

27. McCoy, *Historic Sketches,* p. 139.

28. Hunter, *Trail Drivers,* 1:118.

CHAPTER 4

1. Adams, *Log of a Cowboy,* p. 29. See also Charles Goodnight, "Managing a Trail Herd in the Early Days," *Frontier Times* 6 (November 1929): 250–52.

2. James Henry Cook, *Longhorn Cowboy* (New York: G.P. Putnam's Sons, 1942), p. 101.

3. Cordia Sloan Duke and Joe B. Frantz, *6000 Miles of Fence: Life on the XIT Ranch of Texas* (Austin: University of Texas Press, 1961), p. 81.

4. Abbott and Smith, *We Pointed Them North,* p. 94.

5. Hunter, *Trail Drivers,* 1:314–15.

6. Baylis John Fletcher, *Up the Trail in '79* (Norman: University of Oklahoma Press, 1968), p. 8.

7. Ibid., p. 53.

8. Adams, *Best of the Cowboy,* p. 221.

9. Fletcher, *Up the Trail,* p. 8.

10. Dobie, *Vaquero,* p. 179.

11. J. Frank Dobie, "Ab Blocker: Trail Boss," *Arizona and the West* 6 (Summer 1964): 99.

12. Frank Dalton, "Military Escort for a Trail Herd," *Cattleman* 32 (June 1944): 13–14; Hunter, *Trail Drivers,* 2:704.

13. Hunter, *Trail Drivers,* 1:471.

14. Chris Emmett, *Shanghai Pierce: A Fair Likeness* (Norman: University of Oklahoma Press, 1953), p. 125.

15. Hunter, *Trail Drivers,* 1:128–29.

16. Ibid., pp. 73–75.

17. Adams, *Best of the Cowboy,* p. 225.

CHAPTER 5

1. Walker D. Wyman, *Nothing but Prairie and Sky: Life on the Dakota*

Range in the Early Days (Norman: University of Oklahoma Press, 1954), p. 57.

2. J. Evetts Haley, *Charles Goodnight, Cowman and Plainsman* (Norman: University of Oklahoma Press, 1949), pp. 121–22.

3. Sims, *Cowpokes*, p. 63.

4. Brayer, *American Cattle Trails*, p. 86.

5. Haley, *Charles Goodnight*, p. 93.

6. Fletcher, *Up the Trail*, p. 46.

7. Hunter, *Trail Drivers*, 1:165.

8. Bob Kennon, *From the Pecos to the Powder: A Cowboy's Autobiography*, as told to Ramon F. Adams (Norman: University of Oklahoma Press, 1965), p. 61.

9. Charles A. Siringo, *A Texas Cowboy* (New York: William Sloane Associates, 1950), pp. 77–78.

10. Kennon, *From the Pecos to the Powder*, p. 84.

11. Ibid., p. 87.

12. A. B. Snyder, *Pinnacle Jake*, as told to Nellie Snyder Yost (Lincoln: University of Nebraska Press, 1951), p. 88.

13. Nordyke, *Great Roundup*, p. 62.

14. Sims, *Cowpokes*, p. 63.

15. Brayer, *American Cattle Trails*, p. 110.

16. Courtesy of William F. Bragg, Jr., of Casper, Wyoming.

CHAPTER 6

1. Lewis Atherton, *The Cattle Kings* (Lincoln: University of Nebraska Press, 1972), pp. 5–29; idem, "Cattleman and Cowboy; Fact and Fancy," *Montana, the Magazine of Western History* 11 (October 1961): 2–17.

2. Wyman, *Nothing but Prairie and Sky*, pp. 100–101.

3. John Clay, *My Life on the Range* (Norman: University of Oklahoma Press, 1962), p. 82.

4. Ibid., pp. 122–24.

5. Edward Douglas Branch, *The Cowboy and His Interpreters* (New York: D. Appleton and Co., 1926), pp. 11–12.

6. Mack Williams, *In Old Fort Worth: The Story of a City and Its People as Published in the News-Tribune in 1976 and 1977* (Fort Worth: Williams, 1977), pp. 7–8.

7. Frank S. Hastings, *A Ranchman's Recollections: An Autobiography* (Chicago: Breeder's Gazette, 1921), p. 118.

8. Abbott and Smith, *We Pointed Them North*, pp. 211–12.

9. Adams, *Best of the Cowboy*, pp. 4–5.

10. Ibid., p. 108.

11. Dodge, *Our Wild Indians*, pp. 609, 611.

12. Clifford P. Westermeier, *Man, Beast, Dust: The Story of Rodeo* (n.p.: World Press, 1947), p. 39.

13. See James Henry Cook, *Longhorn Cowboy*, ed. Howard R. Driggs (New York: G. P. Putnam's Sons, 1942); Frank Collinson, *Life in the Saddle*, ed. Mary Whately Clarke (Norman: University of Oklahoma Press, 1963); Baylis John Fletcher, *Up the Trail in '79* (Norman: University of Oklahoma Press, 1968); and E. E. MacConnell, *XIT Buck* (Tucson: University of Arizona Press, 1968).

14. Frazier Hunt, *The Long Trail from Texas: The Story of Ad Spaugh, Cattleman* (New York: Doubleday, Doran and Co., 1940).

15. This and the following quotations, including the tale of the silk hat, are from James, *27 Years a Maverick*, pp. 33–56.

16. O. W. Nolen, "Shanghai Pierce," *Cattleman* 31 (December 1944): 31.

17. Abbott and Smith, *We Pointed Them North*, p. 29.

18. Ibid., pp. 60–61. The following quotation is from the same source, p. 4.

19. Cook, *Longhorn Cowboy*, p. 35.

20. Ibid., pp. 113–14.

21. Kennedy, *Cowboys and Cattlemen*, pp. 115–28.

22. Edgar Beecher Bronson, *Reminiscences of a Ranchman* (Lincoln: University of Nebraska Press, 1962), p. 27.

23. Ibid., pp. 27–28.

24. Ibid., p. 41.

25. Ibid., pp. 46–73.

26. Theodore Roosevelt, *Ranch Life and Hunting Trail* (Ann Arbor: University Microfilms, 1966), p. 62.

27. Quoted from the *Cheyenne Daily Leader*, October 3, 1882, in Westermeier, *Story of Rodeo*, p. 40n.

28. Abbott and Smith, *We Pointed Them North*, pp. 107–9.

29. Edgar Rye, *The Quirt and the Spur: Vanishing Shadows of the Texas Frontier* (Chicago: W. B. Conkey Co., 1909), pp. 271–75.

30. Charles Goodnight, "Managing a Trail Herd," p. 252; see also *History of Montana, 1739–1885* (Chicago: Warner, Beers and Co., 1885), pp. 445–46.

CHAPTER 7

1. John Q. Anderson, ed., *Tales of Frontier Texas, 1830–1860* (Dallas: Southern Methodist University Press, 1966), p. 20.

2. Dobie, *The Longhorns,* p. 35.

3. John J. Linn, *Reminiscences of Fifty Years in Texas* (Austin: Steck Co., 1935), p. 338.

4. Anderson, *Tales of Frontier Texas,* pp. 63–64.

5. Lewis F. Allen, *American Cattle: Their History, Breeding and Management* (New York: Taintor Brothers Co., 1868), pp. 75–84.

6. Benton, *Cow by the Tail,* pp. 65–66.

7. Harry Sinclair Drago, *Red River Valley: The Mainstream of Frontier History from the Louisiana Bayous to the Texas Panhandle* (New York: Clarkson N. Potter, 1962), pp. 181–82.

8. Dobie, *The Longhorns,* pp. 181–4.

9. *Fort Benton Record,* June 23, 1876, in *Montana, the Magazine of Western History* 3 (Autumn 1953): 31.

10. J. L. Hill, *The End of the Cattle Trail* (Austin: Pemberton Press, 1969), pp. 66–67. *Dogie,* from *doughgut,* meant a pot-bellied orphan calf.

11. Gard, "Retracing the Chisholm Trail," p. 55.

12 Joseph Nimmo, Jr., *Report in Regard to the Range and Ranch Cattle Business of the United States* (New York: Arno Press, 1972), pp. 95, 144.

13. Collinson, *Life in the Saddle,* p. 42.

14. Drago, *Red River Valley,* p. 203.

15. Anderson, *Tales of Frontier Texas,* pp. 16–22.

16. Walker D. Wyman, *The Wild Horse of the West* (Caldwell, Idaho: Caxton Printers, 1945), p. 116.

17. Josiah Gregg, *Commerce of the Prairies* (Norman: University of Oklahoma Press, 1954), pp. 126–27.

18. Jordan, "Steinert's View of Texas," p. 46.

19. J. Frank Dobie, *The Mustangs* (New York: Bantam Books, 1954), pp. 82–83.

20. Frederic Remington, "Horses of the Plains," *Century Magazine* 37 (November 1888–April 1889): 335–42.

21. J. Frank Dobie, "The Spanish Cow Pony," *Saturday Evening Post* 207 (November 24, 1934): 13, 65–66.

22. Dobie, *Mustangs,* pp. 293–94. *Pitching* was the term used in the Southwest; *bucking* was used in the North.

23. Ibid., p. 48.

24. Ibid., pp. 161–62.

25. Snyder, *Pinnacle Jake,* pp. 24–32.

26. Malcolm D. McLean, *Fine Texas Horses: Their Pedigrees and Performance, 1830–1845* (Fort Worth: Texas Christian University Press, 1966), p. 82.

27. Wyman, *Wild Horse of the West*, p. 104.
28. Bronson, *Reminiscences*, pp. 153–56.

CHAPTER 8

1. McCoy, *Historic Sketches*, pp. 202–5.
2. Harry Sinclair Drago, *Great American Cattle Trails* (New York: Bramhall House, 1965), p. 140.
3. Ibid., pp. 140–41.
4. Ibid., p. 144.
5. Ibid, pp. 146–47.
6. Ibid., p. 148.
7. Robert R. Dykstra, *The Cattle Towns* (New York: Alfred A. Knopf, 1968), pp. 75–76.
8. Benton, *Cow by the Tail*, pp. 53–57.
9. Stanley Vestal, *Queen of the Cowtowns: Dodge City, "The Wickedest Little City in America," 1872–1886* (Lincoln: University of Nebraska Press, 1972), pp. 3, 86.
10. Harry Sinclair Drago, *Wild, Woolly and Wicked: The History of the Kansas Cow Towns and the Texas Cattle Trail* (New York: Clarkson N. Potter, 1960), p. 235.
11. Ibid., p. 255.
12. Khleber Miller Van Zandt, *Force without Fanfare*, ed. Sandra L. Myres (Fort Worth: Texas Christian University Press, 1968), p. 113.
13. Hunter, *Trail Drivers*, 1:431–32; Taylor, *The Chisholm Trail*, p. 62.
14. Leonard Sanders and Ronnie C. Tyler, *How Fort Worth Became the Texasmost City* (Fort Worth: Amon Carter Museum of Western Art, 1973), p. 36.
15. Ibid., p. 38.
16. Ibid., p. 65.
17. Ibid., p. 68.
18. Ibid.
19. Gard, *The Chisholm Trail*, pp. 217–18.
20. Ibid., p. 234.
21. Ibid., p. 238.
22. Sanders and Tyler, *Fort Worth*, p. 107.

CHAPTER 9

1. Jimmy Skaggs, *The Cattle-Trailing Industry between Supply and*

Demand, 1886–1890 (Lawrence: University of Kansas Press, 1973), pp. 41–44.

2. Ibid., pp. 54–57.
3. Ibid., p. 6.
4. Ibid., p. 1.
5. Ibid., p. 88.
6. Gressley, *Bankers and Cattlemen,* pp. 70, 119. The following direct quotation is from the same source, p. 119.
7. James S. Brisbin, *The Beef Bonanza; or, How to Get Rich on the Plains* (Norman: University of Oklahoma Press, 1959), p. 15.
8. Emmett, *Shanghai Pierce,* pp. 97–109, 154–57, 169–74, 185–90; Gressley, *Bankers and Cattlemen,* p. 77.
9. Gressley, *Bankers and Cattlemen,* p. 71.
10. Ibid., pp. 112–14.
11. Nellie Snyder Yost, ed., *Boss Cowman: The Recollections of Ed Lemmon, 1857–1946* (Lincoln: University of Nebraska Press, 1969), p. 168.
12. William A. Baillie-Grohman, "Cattle Ranches in the Far West," *Library Magazine of American and Foreign Thought* 6 (December 1880): 131.
13. John Clay, *My Life on the Range* (Norman: University of Oklahoma Press, 1962), p. 83.
14. Robert Henry Fletcher, *Free Grass to Fences: The Montana Cattle Range Story* (New York: University Publishers, 1960), pp. 90–91.
15. Gressley, *Bankers and Cattlemen,* p. 135.
16. Gressley, "Harvard Man Out West," p. 20n.
17. William Pearce, *The Matador Land and Cattle Company* (Norman: University of Oklahoma Press, 1964), p. 30.
18. Edward Everett Dale, *The Range Cattle Industry: Ranching on the Great Plains from 1865–1925* (Norman: University of Oklahoma Press, 1960), p. 58n.
19. Clay, *My Life on the Range,* pp. 127–35.
20. E. E. MacConnell, *XIT Buck* (Tucson: University of Arizona Press, 1968), pp. 172–75; Joe B. Frantz, "Texas' Largest Ranch—in Montana: The XIT," *Montana, the Magazine of Western History* 11 (October 1961): 46–56.
21. Clay, *My Life on the Range,* p. 114.
22. Harmon Ross Motherhead, *The Swan Land and Cattle Company, Ltd.* (Norman: University of Oklahoma Press, 1971), pp. 160, 165.
23. Clay, *My Life on the Range,* p. 50.
24. Ibid., pp. 202–4.

25. Gressley, "Harvard Man Out West," pp. 14–16.

26. Clay, *My Life on the Range*, p. 174.

CHAPTER 10

1. Robert H. Burns, "The Newman Brothers: Forgotten Cattle Kings of the Northern Plains," *Montana, the Magazine of Western History* 11 (October 1961): 28–36; Joseph Nimmo, Jr., "The American Cow-Boy," *Harper's New Monthly Magazine* 73 (November 1886): 880–84.

2. Maurice Frink, W. Turrentine Jackson, and Agnes Wright Spring, *When Grass Was King* (Boulder: University of Colorado Press, 1956), p. 36.

3. Granville Stuart, *Pioneering in Montana: The Making of a State, 1864–1887* (Lincoln: University of Nebraska Press, 1977), p. 98; Frink, Jackson, and Spring, *When Grass Was King*, p. 37.

4. Kennedy, *Cowboys and Cattlemen*, pp. 103–8.

5. Fletcher, *Free Grass to Fences*, p. 29.

6. Conrad Kohrs, *An Autobiography* (Deer Lodge, Montana: Plateau Press, 1977), p. 55.

7. Ibid., pp. 43–55; Larry Gill, "From Butcher Boy to Beef King: The Gold Camp Days of Conrad Kohrs," *Montana, the Magazine of Western History* 8 (Spring 1958): 40–55. Today the Kohrs Ranch in Deer Lodge valley is a national park.

8. Frink, Jackson, and Spring, *When Grass Was King*, pp. 336–55.

9. Brisbin, *Beef Bonanza*, pp. 73–74.

10. Ibid., pp. 25–26.

11. Ibid., p. 73.

12. Brayer, *American Cattle Trails*, pp. 33–37.

13. Ibid., pp. 71–76.

14. McCoy, *Historic Sketches*, pp. 342–68.

15. Frink, Jackson, and Spring, *When Grass Was King*, pp. 406–7.

16. Nordyke, *Great Roundup*, p. 90.

17. Wyman, *Nothing but Prairie and Sky*, pp. 58–59.

18. Bronson, *Reminiscences*, p. 75.

19. William MacLeod Raine and Will C. Barnes, *Cattle* (New York: Doubleday, 1930), pp. 233–41.

20. Gressley, *Bankers and Cattlemen*, p. 145.

21. Nordyke, *Great Roundup*, p. 101.

22. Abbott and Smith, *We Pointed Them North*, pp. 137–38.

23. Harold E. Briggs, "The Development and Decline of Open

Range Ranching in the Northwest," *Mississippi Valley Historical Review* 20 (March 1934): 521–22.

24. Bronson, *Reminiscences*, p. 78.
25. Clay, *My Life on the Range*, pp. 72–78.
26. Ibid., p. 53.
27. Gressley, *Bankers and Cattlemen*, p. 68.
28. Roger V. Clements, "British Investment and American Legislative Restrictions in the Trans-Mississippi West, 1880–1900," *Mississippi Valley Historical Review* 42 (September 1955): 207–15.
29. Atherton, *The Cattle Kings*, p. 45.
30. Nordyke, *Great Roundup*, p. 130.
31. Clay, *My Life on the Range*, pp. 177–79.
32. Nordyke, *Great Roundup*, p. 164.
33. Ibid., pp. 168, 185.
34. Andy Adams, *The Outlet* (Upper Saddle River, N.J.: Literature House, 1970), pp. 175–76.
35. Fletcher, *Free Grass to Fences*, p. 91.
36. Kennedy, *Cowboys and Cattlemen*, pp. 156–57.
37. Abbott and Smith, *We Pointed Them North*, p. 175.
38. Ibid., p. 176.
39. Nordyke, *Great Roundup*, pp. 161–62; Wallis Huidekoper, "The Story Behind Charlie Russell's Masterpiece: 'Waiting for a Chinook,' " *Montana, the Magazine of Western History* 4 (Summer 1954): 37–39.
40. Fletcher, *Free Grass to Fences*, p. 92.
41. Kennedy, *Cowboys and Cattlemen*, p. 165.
42. Clay, *My Life on the Range*, p. 200.
43. Abbott and Smith, *We Pointed Them North*, p. 184.
44. Ibid., p. 185.
45. Stuart, *Pioneering in Montana*, pp. 236–37.
46. Quoted in Fletcher, *Free Grass to Fences*, p. 91.
47. Ibid., p. 89.
48. Kennedy, *Cowboys and Cattlemen*, p. 66
49. Kohrs, *Autobiography*, pp. 87–93,
50. Fletcher, *Free Grass to Fences*, p. 93.
51. Robert S. Fletcher, "The End of the Open Range in Eastern Montana," *Mississippi Valley Historical Review* 16 (September 1929): 202–11.
52. Gressley, *Bankers and Cattlemen*, pp. 255–56.
53. Ibid., p. 95.

Bibliography

Books

Abbott, E. C. ("Teddy Blue"), and Smith, Helena Huntington. *We Pointed Them North*. Norman: University of Oklahoma Press, 1954.

Adams, Andy. *The Log of a Cowboy: A Narrative of the Old Trail Days*. 1903. Rpt. Lincoln: University of Nebraska Press, 1964.

————. *The Outlet*. 1905. Rpt. Upper Saddle River, N.J.: Literature House, 1970.

Adams, Ramon F. *The Best of the American Cowboy*. Norman: University of Oklahoma Press, 1957.

————. *Come and Get It*. Norman: University of Oklahoma Press, 1952.

————. *The Old Time Cowhand*. New York: Macmillan Co., 1961.

Allen, Lewis F. *American Cattle: Their History, Breeding and Management*. New York: Taintor Brothers Co., 1868.

Anderson, John Q., ed. *Tales of Frontier Texas, 1830–1860*. Dallas: Southern Methodist University Press, 1966.

Anderson, Oscar Edward, Jr. *Refrigeration in America: A History of a New Technology and Its Impact*. Princeton: Princeton University Press, 1953.

Atherton, Lewis. *The Cattle Kings*. Lincoln: University of Nebraska Press, 1972.

Barnes, Will C. *Apaches and Longhorns: The Reminiscences of Will C. Barnes*. Los Angeles: Ward Ritchie Press, 1941.

Benton, Jesse James. *Cow by the Tail*. Boston: Houghton Mifflin Co., 1943.

Branch, Edward Douglas. *The Cowboy and His Interpreters*. New York: D. Appleton and Co., 1926.

Brayer, Grant M. and Herbert O. *American Cattle Trails, 1540–1900*. Bayside, N.Y.: Western Range Cattle Industry Study in Cooperation with the American Pioneer Trails Society, 1952.

Brisbin, James S. *The Beef Bonanza; or, How to Get Rich on the Plains*. 1881. Rpt. Norman: University of Oklahoma Press, 1959.

Bronson, Edgar Beecher, 1910. Rpt. *Reminiscences of a Ranchman*. Lincoln: University of Nebraska Press, 1962.

Carpenter, Will Tom. *Lucky 7: A Cowman's Autobiography*. Austin: University of Texas Press, 1957.

Clarke, Mary Whately. *A Century of Cow Business: A History of the Texas* and *Southwestern Cattle Raisers Association.* Fort Worth: Texas and Southwestern Cattle Raisers Association, 1976.

Clay, John. *My Life on the Range.* 1924. Rpt. Norman: University of Oklahoma Press, 1962.

Coburn, Walt. *Pioneer Cattleman in Montana: The Story of the Circle C Ranch.* Norman: University of Oklahoma Press, 1968.

Collinson, Frank. *Life in the Saddle.* Edited by Mary Whately Clarke. Norman: University of Oklahoma Press, 1963.

Cook, Harold J. *Tales of the 04 Ranch: Recollections of Harold J. Cook, 1887–1909.* Lincoln: University of Nebraska Press, 1968.

Cook, James Henry. *Fifty Years on the Old Frontier.* New Haven: Yale University Press, 1923.

———. *Longhorn Cowboy.* Edited by Howard R. Driggs. New York: G. P. Putnam's Sons, 1942.

Dale, Edward Everett. *Cow Country.* Norman: University of Oklahoma Press, 1942.

———. *The Range Cattle Industry: Ranching on the Great Plains from 1865 to 1925.* Norman: University of Oklahoma Press, 1960.

Davis, Richard Harding. *The West from a Car-Window.* New York: Harper and Bros., 1892.

Degler, Carl N. *The Age of Economic Revolution, 1876–1900.* Glenview, Ill.: Scott, Foresman, 1967.

Dobie, J. Frank. *Cow People.* Boston: Little, Brown Co., 1964.

———. *The Longhorns.* Boston: Little, Brown Co., 1941.

———. *The Mustangs.* 1934. Rpt. New York: Bantam Books, 1954.

———. *A Vaquero of the Brush Country.* New York: Grosset and Dunlap, 1929.

Dodge, Richard Irving. *Our Wild Indians: Thirty-three Years' Personal Experience among Red Men of the Great West.* Hartford: A. D. Worthington and Co., 1886.

Douglas, C. L. *The Cattle Kings of Texas.* Fort Worth: Branch-Smith, 1968.

Drago, Harry Sinclair. *Great American Cattle Trails.* New York: Bramhall House, 1965.

——— *Red River Valley: The Mainstream of Frontier History from the Louisiana Bayous to the Texas Panhandle.* New York: Clarkson N. Potter, 1962.

———. *Wild, Woolly and Wicked: The History of the Kansas Cow Towns and the Texas Cattle Trail.* New York: Clarkson N. Potter, 1960.

Duke, Cordia Sloan, and Frantz, Joe B., *6000 Miles of Fence: Life on the XIT Ranch of Texas.* Austin: University of Texas Press, 1961.

Dykstra, Robert R. *The Cattle Towns.* New York: Alfred A. Knopf, 1968.

Emmett, Chris. *Shanghai Pierce: A Fair Likeness.* Norman: University of Oklahoma Press, 1953.

Flanagan, Sue. *Trailing the Longhorns a Century Later.* Austin: Madrona Press, 1974.

Fletcher, Baylis John. *Up the Trail in '79.* Norman: University of Oklahoma Press, 1968.

Fletcher, Robert Henry. *Free Grass to Fences: The Montana Cattle Range Story.* New York: University Publishers, 1960.

Foster-Harris. *The Look of the Old West.* New York: Bonanza Books, 1955.

Frantz, Joe B., and Choate, Julian Ernest, Jr. *The American Cowboy: The Myth and the Reality.* Norman: University of Oklahoma Press, 1955.

Frink, Maurice; Jackson, W. Turrentine; and Spring, Agnes Wright. *When Grass Was King.* Boulder: University of Colorado Press, 1956.

Gard, Wayne. *The Chisholm Trail.* Norman: University of Oklahoma Press, 1954.

——. *Reminiscences of Range Life.* Austin: Steck-Vaughn Co., 1970.

Gipson, Frederick B. *Cowhand: The Story of a Working Cowboy.* New York: Harper and Bros., 1948.

Gray, Frank S. *Pioneering in Southwest Texas: True Stories of Early Day Experiences in Edwards and Adjoining Counties.* Edited by Marvin Hunter. Austin: Steck Co., 1949.

Gregg, Josiah. *Commerce of the Prairies.* 1844. Rpt. Norman: University of Oklahoma Press, 1954.

Gressley, Gene M. *Bankers and Cattlemen.* 1966. Rpt. Lincoln: University of Nebraska Press, 1971.

Haley, J. Evetts. *Charles Goodnight, Cowman and Plainsman.* Norman: University of Oklahoma Press, 1949.

——. *George W. Littlefield, Texan.* Norman: University of Oklahoma Press, 1943.

Halsell, Harry H. *Cowboys and Cattleland.* Nashville: Parthenon Press, 1937.

Hamner, Laura V. *Short Grass and Longhorns.* Norman: University of Oklahoma Press, 1943.

Hastings, Frank S. *A Ranchman's Recollections: An Autobiography.* Chicago: Breeder's Gazette, 1921.

Hill, J. L. *The End of the Cattle Trail.* 1924. Rpt. Austin: Pemberton Press, 1969.

History of Montana, 1739–1885. Chicago: Warner, Beers and Co., 1885.

Holden, William Curry. *A Ranching Saga: The Lives of William Electious Halsell and Ewing Halsell.* 2 vols. San Antonio: Trinity University Press, 1976.

192   *Bibliography*

Hudson, Wilson M. *Andy Adams: His Life and Writings.* Dallas: Southern Methodist University Press, 1964.

Hunt, Frazier. *The Long Trail from Texas: The Story of Ad Spaugh, Cattleman.* New York: Doubleday, Doran and Co., 1940.

Hunter, J. Marvin, ed. *The Trail Drivers of Texas.* 2 vols. 1925. Rpt. New York: Argosy-Antiquarian, 1963.

James, Will. *Cowboys North and South.* New York: Charles Scribner's Sons, 1926.

————. *Lone Cowboy.* New York: Charles Scribner's Sons, 1930.

James, Will S. *27 Years a Maverick; or, Life on a Texas Range.* 1893. Rpt. Austin: Steck-Vaughn Co., 1968.

Jones, John Oliver. *A Cowman's Memoirs.* Fort Worth: Texas Christian University Press, 1953.

Kennedy, Michael S., ed. *Cowboys and Cattlemen.* New York: Hastings House, 1964.

Kennon, Bob. *From the Pecos to the Powder: A Cowboy's Autobiography.* As told to Ramon F. Adams. Norman: University of Oklahoma Press, 1965.

Knight, Oliver. *Fort Worth: Outpost on the Trinity.* Norman: University of Oklahoma Press, 1953.

Kohrs, Conrad. *An Autobiography.* Deer Lodge, Montana: Plateau Press, 1977.

Linn, John J. *Reminiscences of Fifty Years in Texas.* 1883. Rpt. Austin: Steck Co., 1935.

McCallum, Henry D. and Frances T. *The Wire That Fenced the West.* Norman: University of Oklahoma Press, 1965.

MacConnell, E. E. *XIT Buck.* Tucson: University of Arizona Press, 1968.

McCoy, Joseph G. *Historic Sketches of the Cattle Trade of the West and Southwest.* 1874. Rpt. Columbus, Ohio: Long's College Book Co., 1951.

McLean, Malcolm D. *Fine Texas Horses: Their Pedigrees and Performance, 1830–1845.* Fort Worth: Texas Christian University Press, 1966.

Marcy, Randolph B. *The Prairie Traveler.* 1859. Rpt. Williamstown, Mass.: Corner House Publishers, 1968.

Motherhead, Harmon Ross. *The Swan Land and Cattle Company, Ltd.* Norman: University of Oklahoma Press, 1971.

Nimmo, Joseph, Jr. *Report in Regard to the Range and Ranch Cattle Business of the United States.* 1885. Rpt. New York: Arno Press, 1972.

Nordyke, Lewis. *Great Roundup: The Story of the Texas and Southwestern Cowmen.* New York: Morrow, 1955.

Olmsted, Frederick Law. *A Journey through Texas; or, A Saddle-Trip on the Southwestern Frontier.* New York: Dix and Edwards, 1857.

Osgood, Ernest Staples. *The Day of the Cattleman.* Minneapolis: University of Minnesota Press, 1954.

Pearce, William. *The Matador Land and Cattle Company.* Norman: University of Oklahoma Press, 1964.

Pelzer, Louis. *The Cattleman's Frontier: A Record of the Trans-Mississippi Cattle Industry from Oxen Trains to Packing Companies, 1850–1890.* Glendale, Calif.: Arthur H. Clark Co., 1936.

Preece, Harold. *Lone Star Man: Ira Aten, Last of the Old Texas Rangers.* New York: Hastings House, 1960.

Raine, William MacLeod, and Barnes, Will C. *Cattle.* New York: Doubleday, 1930.

Richardson, Rupert Norval. *The Frontier of Northwest Texas, 1846 to 1876.* Glendale, Calif.: Arthur H. Clark Co., 1963.

Richthofen, Walter Baron von. 1885. Rpt. *Cattle-Raising on the Plains of North America.* Norman: University of Oklahoma Press, 1964.

Rickey, Don, Jr. *$10 Horse, $40 Saddle: Cowboy Clothing, Arms, Tools and Horse Gear of the 1880's.* Fort Collins, Colo.: Old Army Press, 1976.

Ridings, Sam P. *The Chisholm Trail: A History of the World's Greatest Cattle Trail.* Guthrie, Okla.: Coop Publishers, 1936.

Roach, Joyce Gibson. *The Cowgirls.* Houston: Cordovan Corporation, 1977.

Rollins, Philip Ashton. *The Cowboy: His Characteristics, His Equipment, and His Part in the Development of the West.* New York: Charles Scribner's Sons, 1926.

Roosevelt, Theodore. *Ranch Life and Hunting Trail.* Ann Arbor, Mich.: University Microfilms, 1966.

Rye, Edgar. *The Quirt and the Spur: Vanishing Shadows of the Texas Frontier.* Chicago: W. B. Conkey Co., 1909.

Sanders, Leonard, and Tyler, Ronnie C. *How Fort Worth Became the Texasmost City.* Fort Worth: Amon Carter Museum of Western Art, 1973.

Sandoz, Mari. *The Cattlemen, from the Rio Grande across the Far Marias.* New York: Hastings House, 1958.

Savage, William W., Jr., ed. *Cowboy Life: Reconstructing an American Myth.* Norman: University of Oklahoma Press, 1975.

Sims, Orland L. *Cowpokes, Nesters, and so Forth.* Austin: Encino Press, 1970.

Siringo, Charles A. *A Texas Cowboy; or, Fifteen Years on the Hurricane Deck of a Spanish Pony.* 1886. Rpt. New York: William Sloane Assoc., 1950.

Skaggs, Jimmy. *The Cattle-Trailing Industry: Between Supply and Demand, 1866–1890.* Lawrence: University of Kansas Press, 1973.

Smith, Helena Huntington. *The War on the Powder River.* Lincoln: University of Nebraska Press, 1967.

Snyder, A. B. *Pinnacle Jake.* As told to Nellie Snyder Yost. Lincoln: University of Nebraska Press, 1951.

Sonnichsen, C. L. *Cowboys and Cattle Kings.* Norman: University of Oklahoma Press, 1950.

———. *From Hopalong to Hud.* College Station: Texas A & M University Press, 1978.

Stone, William Hale. *Twenty-Four Years a Cowboy and Ranchman in Southern Texas and Old Mexico.* Norman: University of Oklahoma Press, 1959.

Streeter, Floyd Benjamin. *Prairie Trails and Cow Towns: The Opening of the Old West.* New York: Devin Adair, 1963.

Stuart, Granville. *Pioneering in Montana: The Making of a State, 1864–1887.* 1925. Rpt. Lincoln: University of Nebraska Press, 1977.

Taylor, Thomas Ulvan. *The Chisholm Trail and Other Routes.* San Antonio: Naylor Co., 1936.

Van Zandt, Khleber Miller. *Force without Fanfare.* Edited by Sandra L. Myres. Fort Worth: Texas Christian University Press, 1968.

Verckler, Stewart P. *Cowtown-Abilene: The Story of Abilene, Kansas, 1867–1875.* New York: Carlton Press, 1961.

Vestal, Stanley. *Queen of Cowtowns: Dodge City, "The Wickedest Little City in America," 1872–1886.* 1952. Rpt. Lincoln: University of Nebraska Press, 1972.

Ward, Don, ed. *Bits of Silver: Vignettes of the Old West.* New York: Hastings House, 1961.

Ward, Fay E. *The Cowboy at Work.* New York: Hastings House, 1958.

Westermeier, Clifford P. *Man, Beast, Dust: The Story of Rodeo.* N.P.: World Press, 1947.

Williams, Mack. *In Old Fort Worth: The Story of a City and Its People as Published in the News-Tribune in 1976 and 1977.* Fort Worth: Williams, 1977.

Wyman, Walker D. *Nothing but Prairie and Sky: Life on the Dakota Range in the Early Days.* Norman: University of Oklahoma Press, 1954.

———. *The Wild Horse of the West.* Caldwell, Idaho: Caxton Printers, 1945.

Yost, Nellie Snyder., ed. *Boss Cowman: The Recollections of Ed Lemmon, 1857–1946.* Lincoln: University of Nebraska Press, 1969.

ARTICLES

Armitage, George T. "Prelude to the Last Great Roundup: The Dying Days of the Great 79." *Montana, the Magazine of Western History* 11 (October 1961): 66–75.

Ashton, John. "Texas Cattle Trade in 1870." *Cattleman* 38 (July 1951): 21, 74–75.

Atherton, Lewis. "Cattleman and Cowboy: Fact and Fancy," *Montana, the Magazine of Western History* 11 (October 1961): 2–17.

Baillie-Grohman, William A. "Cattle Ranches in the Far West." *Library Magazine of American and Foreign Thoughts* 6 (December 1880): 112–31. Reprinted from the *Fortnightly Review* n.s. 28 (July–December 1880): 438–57.

"Barbed Wire Has Its Place in History." *Frontier Times* 16 (September 1939): 534–35.

Bell, James G. "A Log of the Texas-California Cattle Trail, 1854." Edited by J. Evetts Haley. *Southwestern Historical Quarterly* 35 (January 1932): 208–37; (April 1932): 290–311.

Briggs, Harold E. "The Development and Decline of Open Range Ranching in the Northwest." *Mississippi Valley Historical Review* 20 (March 1934): 521–36.

Brown, Mark H. "New Focus on the Sioux War: Barrier to the Cattlemen." *Montana, the Magazine of Western History* 11 (October 1961): 76–85.

Burns, Robert H. "The Newman Brothers: Forgotten Cattle Kings of the Northern Plains." *Montana, the Magazine of Western History* 11 (October 1961): 28–36.

"Chisholm Cattle Trails in Texas Preserved by Writers." *Frontier Times* 7 (September 1930): 554–55.

Clements, Roger V. "British Investment and American Legislative Restrictions in the Trans-Mississippi West, 1880–1900." *Mississippi Valley Historical Review* 42 (September 1955): 207–28.

Dalton, Frank. "Military Escort for a Trail Herd." *Cattleman* 32 (July 1944): 13–14.

Dobie, J. Frank. "Ab Blocker: Trail Boss." *Arizona and the West* 6 (Summer 1964): 97–103.

———. "The First Cattle in Texas and the Southwest Progenitors of the Longhorns." *Southwestern Historical Quarterly* 42 (January 1939): 171–97.

———. "The Spanish Cow Pony." *Saturday Evening Post* 207 (November 24, 1934): 12–13, 64–66.

————. "Tom Candy Ponting's Drive of Texas Cattle to Illinois." *Cattleman* 35 (January 1949): 34–45.

Doran, Michael. "Antebellum Cattle Herding in the Indian Territory." *Geographical Review* 66 (January 1976): 48–58.

"A Drive from Texas to North Dakota." *Frontier Times* 3 (April 1926): 1–4.

Earhart, E. P. "Up the Cattle Trail in 1867." *Frontier Times* 8 (February 1931): 194–95.

"Early Texas Cattle Industry." *Frontier Times* 5 (September 1928): 476–81.

Fellows, Fred. "Illustrated Study of Western Saddles." *Montana, the Magazine of Western History* 16 (January 1966): 57–83.

"The First Cattle Ranch in Texas." *Frontier Times* 13 (March 1936): 304–8.

Fletcher, Robert H. "The Day of the Cattleman Dawned Early—in Montana." *Montana, the Magazine of Western History* 11 (October 1961): 22–28.

Fletcher, Robert S. "The End of the Open Range in Eastern Montana." *Mississippi Valley Historical Review* 16 (September 1929): 188–211.

Frantz, Joe B. "Texas' Largest Ranch—in Montana: The XIT." *Montana, the Magazine of Western History* 11 (October 1961): 46–56.

Gard, Wayne. "The Fence-Cutters." *Southwestern Historical Quarterly* 51 (July 1947): 1–15.

————. "The Impact of the Cattle Trails." *Southwestern Historical Quarterly* 71 (July 1967): 1–6.

————. "Retracing the Chisholm Trail." *Southwestern Historical Quarterly* 60 (July 1956): 53–68.

Gibson, Arrell M. "The Cowboy in Indian Territory." *Red River Valley Historical Review* 2 (Spring 1975): 147–61.

Gill, Larry. "From Butcher Boy to Beef King: The Gold Camp Days of Conrad Kohrs." *Montana, the Magazine of Western History* 8 (Spring 1958): 40–55.

Gillett, James B. "Beef Gathering in '71 Was Thrilling." *Frontier Times* 3 (April 1926): 6–7.

Goodnight, Charles. "Managing a Trail Herd in the Early Days." *Frontier Times* 6 (November 1929): 250–52.

"Goodnight Sets Out upon 'New Adventure.'" *Frontier Times* 5 (October 1927): 28–30.

Gressley, Gene M., ed. "Harvard Man Out West: The Letters of Richard Trimble, 1882–1887." *Montana, the Magazine of Western History* 10 (Winter 1960): 14–23.

Grove, Fred. "The Old Chisholm Trail." *Oklahoma Today,* Autumn 1966, pp. 24–27.

Guice, John D. "Cattle Raisers of the Old Southwest: A Reinterpretation." *Western Historical Quarterly* 8 (April 1977): 167–88.

Haley, J. Evetts. "And Then Came Barbed Wire to Change History's Course." *Cattleman* 13 (March 1927): 78–83.

Halsell, H. H. "My Chronicle of the Old West." *Cattleman* 38 (August 1957): 98–102.

Harger, Charles Moreau. "Cattle-Trails of the Prairies." *Scribner's Magazine* 11 (June 1892): 732–42.

Hayter, Earl W. "Barbed Wire Fencing—A Prairie Invention." *Agricultural History* 13 (October 1939): 189–207.

Herrington, George Squires. "An Early Cattle Drive from Texas to Illinois." *Southwestern Historical Quarterly* 55 (October 1951): 267–69.

"Hige Nail, an Early Trail Driver." *Frontier Times* 4 (November 1926): 16.

Hollon, Gene. "Captain Charles Schreiner, the Father of the Hill Country." *Southwestern Historical Quarterly* 48 (October 1944): 145–68.

Holt, Roy D. "Fence Cutting War." *Cattleman* 61 (July 1974): 124–26.

————. "From Trail to Rail in Texas Cattle Industry." *Cattleman* 18 (March 1932): 50–59.

————. "Introducing Barbed Wire to Texas Stockmen." *Cattleman* 17 (July 1930): 26–31.

————. "The Introduction of Barbed Wire Into Texas and the Fence Cutting War." *West Texas Historical Association Year Book* 6 (June 1930): 65–79.

Houston, Dunn. "A Drive from Texas to North Dakota." *Frontier Times* 3 (April 1926): 1–4.

Huffman, Adolph. "A Long Dry Drive on the Cattle Trail." *Frontier Times* 8 (May 1940): 335–36.

Huidekoper, Wallis. "The Story Behind Charlie Russell's Masterpiece: 'Waiting for a Chinook.' " *Montana, the Magazine of Western History* 4 (Summer 1954): 37–39.

Hunter, J. Marvin. "George Saunders' First Trip." *Frontier Times* 5 (May 1928): 321–24.

Hutchinson, W. H. "The Cowboy and Karl Marx." *Pacific Historian* 20 (Summer 1976): 111–22.

"Introducing Barbed Wire in Texas." *Frontier Times* 9 (November 1931): 90–92.

Jordan, Gilbert J., tr. and ed. "W. Steinert's View of Texas in 1849," pt. 5. *Southwestern Historical Quarterly* 81 (July 1977): 45–77.

Jordan, Philip D. "The Pistol Packin' Cowboy: From Bullet to Burial." *Red River Valley Historical Review* 2 (Spring 1975): 65–91.

Jordan, Terry G. "Windmills in Texas." *Agricultural History* 37, no. 2 (1961): 80–85.

"The Justin Boot." *Montana, the Magazine of Western History* 11 (January 1961): 86–88.

Keese, J. Pomeroy. "Beef." *Harper's New Monthly Magazine* 69 (July 1884): 292–301.

Kennedy, Michael, ed. "Judith Basin Top Hand: Reminiscences of William Burnett, an Early Montana Cattleman." *Montana, the Magazine of Western History* 3 (Spring 1953): 18–23.

Lunsford, John R. "E. B. Baggett Speaks of Chisholm Trail." *Frontier Times* 8 (December 1930): 127–28.

McCaleb, J. L. "A Texas Boy's First Experience on the Trail." *Frontier Times* 5 (October 1927): 10–13.

Morris, W. J. "Over the Old Chisholm Trail." *Frontier Times* 2 (April 1925): 41–43.

Nimmo, Joseph, Jr. "The American Cow-Boy." *Harper's New Monthly Magazine* 73 (November 1886): 880–84.

Nolen, O. W. "Shanghai Pierce." *Cattleman* 31 (December 1944): 31.

Nunn, Annie Dyer. "Over the Goodnight and Loving Trail." *Frontier Times* 2 (November 1924): 4–7.

"Old Cowman Tells of a Big Steal." *Frontier Times* 3 (June 1926): 36–37.

"An Old Time Cattle Inspector." *Frontier Times* 3 (March 1926): 44–45.

Padgitt, James T. "Colonel William H. Day: Texas Ranchman." *Southwestern Historical Quarterly* 53 (April 1950): 347–66.

Pattie, Jane. "The Justin Boot: Standard of the West." *Quarter Horse Journal* 29 (September 1977): 124–32.

Potter, Jack. "Up the Trail (and Back) in '82." *Montana, the Magazine of Western History* 11 (October 1961): 57–65.

Remington, Frederic. "Horses of the Plains." *Century Magazine* 37 (November 1888–April 1889): 332–43.

Richardson, Ernest M. "John Bull in the Cowmen's West: Moreton Frewen, Cattle King with a Monocle." *Montana, the Magazine of Western History* 11 (October 1961): 37–45.

Russell, Don. "The Cowboy: From Black Hat to White." *Red River Valley Historical Review* 2 (Spring 1975): 13–23.

Sanders, A. Collatt. "Adventures on the Old Cattle Trail." *Frontier Times* 3 (July 1926): 1–3.

Savage, William W., Jr. "The Cowboy Myth." *Red River Valley Historical Review* 2 (Spring 1975): 162–71.

Shelton, Emily Jones. "Lizzie Johnson: A Cattle Queen of Texas." *Southwestern Historical Quarterly* 50 (April 1947): 349–66.

Sinclair, F. H. (Neckyoke Jones). "Down the Trail with a Range Rider." *Montana, the Magazine of Western History* 16 (Summer 1966): 56–64.

Stephens, R. M. "Recollections of a Texas Cowpuncher." *Frontier Times* 2 (July 1925): 11.

Streeter, Floyd Benjamin. "The National Cattle Trail." *Cattleman* 38 (June 1951): 26–27, 59–74.

Taylor, T. U. "Original Chisholm Trail." *Frontier Times* 8 (February 1931): 195–99.

"A Vivid Story of Trail Driving Days." *Frontier Times* 2 (July 1925): 20–23.

Welsh, Donald H. "Cosmopolitan Cattle King: Pierre Wibaux and the W Bar Ranch." *Montana, the Magazine of Western History* 5 (Spring 1955): 1–15.

Westermeier, Clifford P. "Cowboy Sexuality: A Historical No-No?" *Red River Valley Historical Review* 2 (Spring 1975): 93–113.

Wilkeson, Frank. "Cattle Raising on the Plains." *Harper's Monthly Magazine* 72 (1886): 285–96.

Wilson, Glen O. "Old Red River Station." *Southwestern Historical Quarterly* 61 (January 1958): 350–58.

Index